Bert Weteringe

Down Wind

The impact of large-scale
energy production using wind turbines

© 2024 Obelisk Books – part of Obelisk Media B.V., The Netherlands
Dutch original, "Windhandel", August 2023

Cover: San Gorgonio Pass Wind Park, Palm Springs, California.

Down Wind | Bert Weteringe
The impact of large-scale energy production using wind turbines

First print, February 2024

ISBN: 978-94-611-34-2
NUR: 973
info@obeliskboeken.nl

Any part of this book may only be reproduced, stored in a retrieval system and/or transmitted in any form, by print, photo print, microfilm, recording, or other means, chemical, electronic or mechanical, with the written permission of the publisher.

Table of contents

6	Foreword | Dr Coen Vermeeren
9	Introduction

12 Chapter 1: History of the windmill
- 13   Applications of wind and water mills
- 14   The new industrial revolution

19 Chapter 2: Wind turbines for generating energy
- 19   The operating principle of the wind turbine
- 22   The structure of the wind turbine
- 26   The rotor blades
- 26   The foundation of wind turbines
- 28   Piling in the seabed
- 30   Raw materials and mining

40 Chapter 3: Climate policy and the implications for society
- 40   Agenda 21
- 41   Agenda 2030
- 41   The United Nations Sustainable Development Goals
- 42   European Green Deal
- 43   Dutch climate policy
- 44   Regional Energy Strategy
- 46   How many wind turbines do we actually need?
- 48   Oudeschip, East Groningen, The Netherlands
- 50   The consequences of Dutch climate policy

55 Chapter 4: Climate change?
- 55   Code red for climate
- 56   Al Gore
- 58 CO_2 and the climate
- 60   The IPCC
- 61   The logic

65 Chapter 5: Economic aspects of wind turbines
- 65   The cost of construction, installation and operation of wind turbines
- 66   Operation
- 67   System costs
- 71   Unforeseen costs
- 71   Energy revenues and subsidization
- 73   Decreasing wind strength
- 75   Contribution to economic growth
- 75   Wind farm investors

75	Carbon credits
77	Understanding climate spending
78	Impact of wind energy on the power grid
79	The reliability of the current network
82	What all this means for your wallet

86 Chapter 6: The effects of wind turbines on people and nature

86	Forest damage
88	Birds, bats and insects
89	Effects on birds
93	Effect on bats
94	Measures for populations
95	Effects on insects
96	The North Sea: from nature to industrial wind field
98	Impact on humpback whales on the U.S. East Coast
99	Disturbances caused by cabling on the seabed
101	Weather and climate influence by wind turbines
104	Acoustic pollution
105	Dropshadow
106	Decline in value of homes
107	SF6 for electrical insulation
109	Bisphenol-A
111	Other risks around wind turbines
113	Visualizing the effects of overdue maintenance
115	Use and leakage of synthetic oil
115	Wind Turbine Waste
117	Competing interests

122	Thank you
123	Configurative glossary
125	Read more
125	Photos
127	About the author

Foreword

In January 2022, Frans Timmermans, Euro Commissioner for Climate, was awarded an honorary doctorate from TU Delft by Rector President Tim van der Hagen. This high honor was bestowed upon our Dutchman in Brussels because of "his merits in the field of climate." The enormous criticism for awarding him an honorary doctorate came mainly from graduates of Delft University of Technology, who felt that their alma mater was risking its credibility in this way. The more than 23,000 signatures on a petition against the award were to no avail: Frans Timmermans became an honorary doctor, and not only at TU Delft, but a month and a half later also at the University of Ghent.

It immediately outlines the deep interconnectedness between politics and science. After all, the energy transition involves tens of billions of euros a year in the Netherlands and Belgium alone, and neither our politicians, business nor universities and research institutes are averse to that.

In 2019, this same TU Delft had in its climate mission statement that "there is *no doubt*" that humans are responsible for climate change. This pronouncement has nothing to do with science but everything to do with politics. The university received so much criticism for it that they decided to amend it in 2022, at the same time as the honorary doctorate issue. Resistance within science itself, where there was wholehearted support for that climate mission, is almost completely absent. As a result, it is becoming increasingly clear that universities are doing less and less science and more and more politics.

Bert Weteringe was working as a composite materials specialist at the Faculty of Aerospace Engineering in Delft in 2000-2006, the same time I was a lecturer there. As I suggested above, our technical universities are not in all respects the best place at present for technological developments that serve the planet. So, I was pleasantly surprised when he contacted me again after years to say that he was working on a book about wind energy. During our time together in Delft, wind energy was booming, and because of the aerodynamics of the blades, our faculty was the place to develop that technology. Because of the enormous size, the faculty of Civil Engineering was also used for testing the turbine blades. In other words: Delft was and is all about wind energy. Incidentally, wind energy was something that, in the early days, we never imagined would have to lead to the solution to the global energy problem. It was a marginal concept that for certain locations could be a possible (temporary) solution for energy supply, nothing more. So many years on, we know better.

As becomes clear in this book, energy from wind is something we should label "planetarily suicidal technology". Technology that really should never have been developed. Because as soon as a certain technology structurally leads to the annual death of millions of birds, bats, insects and marine animals (people?) - and causes major social nuisance - noise, drop shadow, horizon pollution - then you know one thing for sure: this is not a solution to anything but a gigantic problem. A problem that, if it is up to the transition commissioners, is going to get much, much bigger in the coming years. We absolutely should not want this. This must stop.

Besides, most readers know by now that the problem for which wind turbines are supposed to be the solution does not exist at all. The climate changes by definition and man, with all his invested billions, has exactly "0.00036 °C" influence on it, as our Minister of Climate and Energy so clearly stated. In Delft, by the way, this used to be called 0° and that is awfully close to reality. Pollution from fossil fuels - extraction and use - is an entirely different matter, but then we should also count the wind industry as a heavily polluting industry. So, we have to stop both. And we can, but that is not yet widely recognized.

Because a common argument for wind energy (and solar energy: which is a story apart) is that we have no other choice. But that too is false, which is why I was glad that Bert mentions 'free energy' at the end of his book as an alternative to wind energy - and, I am convinced, the only alternative. Free energy, zero-point energy, vacuum energy or *Radiant Energy* as Nikola Tesla called it 100 years ago, is energy from the fabric of spacetime, the ether. Heavily denied and contested by mainstream science, free energy is little by little seeping into the public domain. This is partly because "unidentified flying objects" are increasingly in the news. Objects that, according to witnesses, "flout all the laws of nature (of transportation and energy)."

Is it a coincidence that this is all happening in our time? No. A developing planetary civilization logically gets more and more need for energy. Of course, this can and should never be at the expense of the planetary inhabitants and the planet itself. After all, let's face it, a society that has ambition and is about to travel to other planets cannot depend on whether it is windy for its transportation and stove, can it? The Creator designed other solutions and all of us, inhabitants of this beautiful planet Earth, in this unimaginable Universe, are now more than ready for it.

I wish the reader much inspiration in reading this book, and I hope he will agree with the author and me that wind energy is not the way forward in any case. It is up to all of us to literally put a stop to unsound technology, no matter how hard it is pushed. Therefore, please share this information with as many others as possible and in addition, if you can, delve into real solutions, such as free energy, that will actually move humanity forward.

Dr Coen Vermeeren

Introduction

Our modern economy is based on reliable and cheap energy. The energy transition initiated by the United Nations means that the economy is going to depend on wind and solar as main sources of energy.

In the process, the motivation behind the energy transition from fossil fuels to solar and wind has changed over the years. Whereas in the 1970s and 1980s it was still thought that there would be a great shortage of fossil fuels, it is now clear that there are sufficient reserves available. So, the current energy transition has nothing to do with a shortage of fossil fuels but is driven by the desire to combat climate change.

An electrification of society has been initiated with the goal of reducing CO_2 emissions for future generations. The motivation for this is that CO_2 has been identified by governments as causing climate change. Man is said to be guilty of this and so man will have to do something about it. One part of the energy transition is the generation of electricity using wind turbines. From a cultural and historical perspective, the Netherlands has a rich history when it comes to windmills, which have traditionally been man's workhorses and thus became an important part of the Dutch cultural landscape. These windmills currently attract many hundreds of thousands, mostly foreign tourists, every year.

Unlike wind*mills* of up to about 20-30 meters in height, the new wind *turbines* are of a very different caliber. Modern wind turbines reach tip heights as high as 260 meters, making them more than prominent in the landscape. Whereas tourists used to come to admire the beautiful Dutch, balanced landscape with its classic wind turbines, the same tourists are not too keen on looking at a horizon with dozens, sometimes even hundreds, of modern wind turbines.

Famous Dutch windmills at the Dutch town of Kinderdijk.

This book begins with a bit of primal Dutch history of the windmill and then quickly moves on to the development of the first wind turbines, machines designed purely to generate energy. In addition to the development and use of this technology, the why of the energy transition is discussed. This has primarily become a prelude to the rise of all kinds of financial markets, particularly around CO_2. To understand the background of the entire energy transition - of which the excessive increase in the construction of wind farms is an important part - I first inform you extensively about the policy pursued and its motivation. In this book, I pay close attention to the harmful effects on humans and nature caused by the construction, installation and use, and removal of wind turbines. All these harmful effects, in addition to the dangers that occur during operation, are explained with practical examples. I deliberately do not use the widely misused word "sustainable" in this book. The reason why will automatically become clear as you read.

Finally, using practical examples, I also discuss exactly what climate policy means for your wallet.

A book about the impact of large-scale energy generation with wind turbines comes not a moment too soon. Since government plans for the energy transition will entail far-reaching changes for the landscape and society, it was about time to inform the public about the background of the energy transition, a transition that is primarily focused on wind energy in the Netherlands, both on land and at sea. The coverage of this, through our public broadcasters and mainstream newspapers, has become increasingly one-sided and incomplete over the past decades. Therefore, it is quite possible that after reading this book, you may look differently at the energy transition in general, and wind turbines in particular. My advice is to continue your own research after reading the book, to look for subjects that have aroused your interest, but especially those subjects where you have doubts whether the information I have presented is correct or not. To help you do this, I have included several references at the end of each chapter. That list, given the enormity of the subject, is obviously not complete. However, with the search terms in this book, you can do an excellent job.

Hopefully, after reading this book, you will agree with me that it is of utmost importance that the information in this book be widely disseminated. After all, as plans for wind energy continue to be realized toward 2050, the damage to the environment - flora and fauna - will begin to increase exponentially. Sharing information about the negative aspects of this *wind trade* is crucial. Only together can we turn back from the dead-end road we have taken.

This book uses several Dutch-language sources and largely reflects the situation around wind policy in the Netherlands. However, the book also contains several examples from other countries and provides a picture of the world situation regarding energy transition.
Where possible, source references have been considered in the translation. However, several Dutch sources were incorporated into the translation.

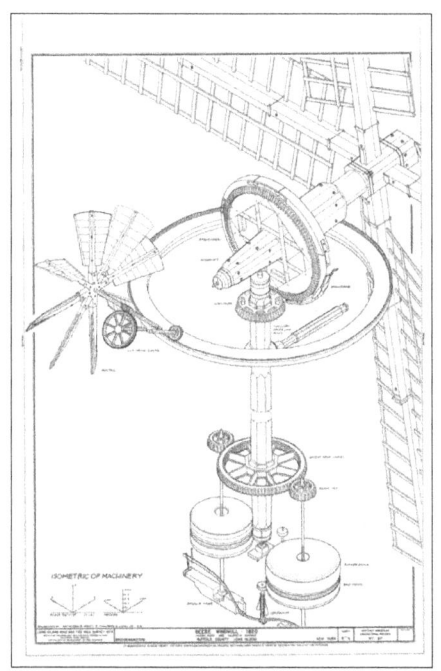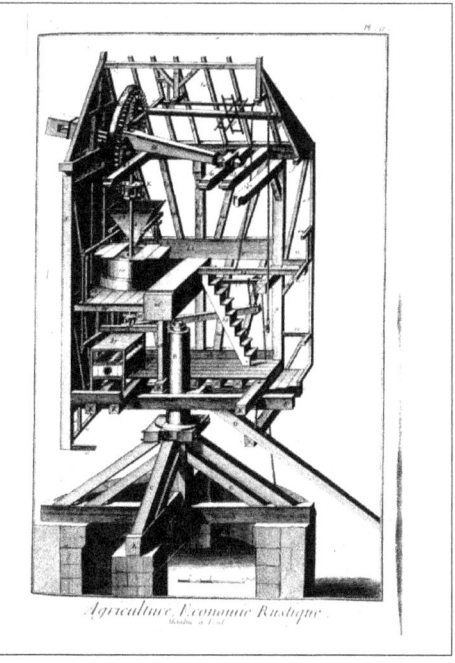
Brilliant and sustainable wind turbine technology in wood.

Chapter 1: History of the windmill

The windmill has a long history.[1] More than 900 years ago, medieval Europe became the first major civilization not to rely entirely on human (and animal) muscle power. Tens of thousands of windmills and watermills revolutionized industry and society. Wind but also water mills were essentially the first true factories. They consisted of a building, machinery, a source of energy (wind or water) and workers. From each of those factories came a product.

Windmills and water wheels were not an invention of the Middle Ages - they already existed in antiquity. The mills of the early Middle Ages were little or no different from them in technical terms. However, ancient civilizations, such as those of the Greeks and Romans, hardly used wind and water technology. It is not clear what reasons were behind this. Perhaps the enormous potential of slave labor was sufficient.

Water-powered mills were generally more important and therefore more numerous than windmills. Hydropower is more reliable than wind power. Although the flow of a river may vary according to the season, generally a river always contains water. Moreover, by cleverly constructing canals and locks, the supply of water along the wheel could be matched exactly to the plant's power requirements.

Besides the fact that sufficient wind is not always guaranteed, wind direction and wind speed vary continuously. Ancient windmills did not have efficient methods for dealing with this. Water-powered mills find their rise in Europe especially at the end of the 11th century. However, not every location is suitable for harvesting energy from flowing water.

Fig. 1.1: An example of a water mill (Stichting Leudal).

There are several reasons for this. For example, if there is insufficient water, as in Spain. If the land has too little elevation, as in the Netherlands and certain parts of England. Also, when streams and rivers freeze over during a long winter, as in Scandinavia, Russia, and parts of Germany. In all these countries, the first windmills appeared in the 13th century, sometimes earlier. In later centuries, windmills were also built in areas that had waterpower.

Applications of wind and water mills

Wind and water mills were used for a variety of industrial processes. In the early days, most mills were used for grinding grain, pumping water and, especially in the Netherlands, draining low-lying areas. For the latter application, windmills, the so-called "polder mills," were connected to an "inverted" water wheel or "scoop wheel," or to a so-called Archimedes' screw.

For the common man, grains were the major component of the medieval diet. Meat, fish, and vegetables were mainly for the wealthy. Grinding all that grain with a hand mill, however, was a time-consuming and labor-intensive job. One person spent two hours a day grinding enough grain for a family. The labor that a large windmill could provide was enough for an entire community, leaving plenty of time for other work. Grinding grain remained the main use of windmills. Well into the 1900s, the entire wheat harvest of northern Europe was milled by windmills in Holland, Denmark, and Germany.

Fig. 1.2 Archimedes' screw.

From 1600, windmills appeared for numerous new applications. For example, in the production of gin. Wind-powered mills were also used for husking barley and rice; milling malt; pressing olives into olive oil and pressing rapeseed and hemp seed; oils used in food preparation but also for lighting. There were cocoa mills, mustard mills, tobacco mills, pepper mills and mills used for other spices.

Two major industrial uses of windmills were to produce paper and sawing wood. Other mills were used for pulverizing lime; for producing cement, grinding mortar, draining mines, ventilating mine shafts, polishing glass and making gunpowder.

Textiles was yet another industry where wind power was used: windmills were used for grinding flax seed to make linen; preparing hemp fibers to produce rope and sailcloth; for "fulling" textiles, to make soft wool; the production of dye and the tanning and coloring of animal hides.

Fig. 1.3: An old windmill.

One of the most spectacular developments of industrial windmills worldwide took place in the Zaan, the region just above Amsterdam. Several factors played a role in this revolutionary development in the Zaan region. It was - and still is - a wet region with swampy soil. As a result, there was probably not enough agricultural work for the entire Zaan population as early as the 15th century. The excess labor force migrated to Amsterdam, went sailing on fishing and trading ships or went into the industry. The proximity of Amsterdam was crucial for the Zaan region, especially its position as a world trade center from the end of the 16th century. The Zaan region could benefit from this and take over services that could not be provided directly in Amsterdam because of the lack of space and the guilds in Amsterdam. In the Zaanstreek these restrictions did not apply, making labor cheaper. In addition, it often proved cheaper for Amsterdam merchants to have their products produced in the Zaan region. What was necessary for this was the invention of the industrial windmill. The first Dutch windmill placed in the Zaan region was an industrial sawmill. Although the area is surrounded by water, the potential for water mills there was limited because the land is as flat as a billiard sheet. But there is wind. Many of the industrial uses of windmills described above first appeared - and sometimes exclusively - in the Zaan. In fact, the region was the world's first industrial park. From 1600 to 1750, when Holland was a major economic power, about a thousand windmills were built here.

A vital element of the wind-powered industry in the Zaan was the sawmill. That wood was needed to build houses, ships, locks, and of course even more windmills. Sawing tree trunks by hand was very time-consuming work. Sawmills saved an enormous amount of time. For example, with a hand saw it took two working days to saw one tree trunk into planks, while with wind power it took only 30 to 40 minutes.

Fig 1.4: The sawing tool in an old-fashioned sawmill.

The new industrial revolution

In the nineteenth century, large-scale production with windmills came to an end. In fact, the invention of the electric generator and the alternating current motor in the 19th century marked the beginning of a new industrial revolution. At first, the production of electricity still required wind power. The very first windmill to generate electric energy was a huge machine with as many as 144 blades. It was built in 1888 by the American Charles Brush in his own backyard. Contrary to what you might think of such a colossus, at full power it produced only 12 kilowatts, which Brush used primarily to light his home in Cleveland.

Brush was followed by Danish physicist Poul Lacour, who in 1891 built a windmill that generated electric power, the so-called wind turbine. Lacour began training electrical mechanics and even set up a wind turbine factory. Denmark became a pioneer in wind-generated electricity, and by 1900 there were hundreds of such wind turbines in the country. However, the demand for electricity grew faster than the supply. With the advent of the steam engine - and later fossil-fuel-powered engines - wind turbines lost many of their traditional roles in the twentieth century. Nor were wind turbines yet in demand. They still did not provide enough electricity in the 20th century, while the demand for electricity at that time was taking a huge leap. That demand, as we know, was met for decades mainly by fossil fuels: coal, oil, and gas.

Fig. 1.5: The very first wind turbine to generate electrical power: Charles Brush in 1888.

Only after the Club of Rome's 1972 report "The Limits to Growth" and the 1973 oil crisis, awareness began to grow of how dependent humanity had become on oil. The government made subsidies available to experiment with alternative sources of energy. Wind power suddenly became interesting again.

In Tvind, Denmark, the first European megawatt wind turbine rose as early as 1977. Slowly, the rest of Europe joined in. Germany was the first to follow Denmark's example by investing in wind energy and installing small wind turbines. The first turbines were about 10 meters high and generated no more than 10 kilowatts of energy. Then, in the 1980s and 1990s, medium-sized wind turbines appeared with an axle height of about 25 to 30 meters.

In 1982, the Netherlands had eleven manufacturers and twelve importers of wind turbines (or parts thereof). Our country now still has one wind turbine manufacturer, the company Lagerwey in Barneveld, which traditionally manufactured two-bladed, but now also three-bladed turbines. In contrast to the Netherlands, Germany and Denmark have a sizeable wind industry.[2] In Germany, the governments of the federal states - each state has its own government there that makes decisions about energy supply - have always been very supportive of wind energy and have also supported that industry financially.

With the use of increasingly taller towers and larger rotor blades, wind turbines are delivering more and more electrical power. Today, wind turbines are being built that can generate up to 12 MW of power, such as the Haliade X from manufacturer General Electric (GE). [3]

But not only are the sizes of the turbines increasing, so are their numbers. In 1990 the Netherlands had only 323 wind turbines, by 2016 there were 2041 and by the end of 2020 the counter stood at 2606 wind turbines, used specifically to produce electricity. Of these, 2,144 were on land - including turbines on inland waters, such as the IJsselmeer - and 462 at sea. In that year, 15.3 billion kWh of electricity was supplied by all these wind turbines. Of that, 36 percent was produced by offshore wind turbines and 64 percent by wind turbines located on land. In 2021, production rose to 17.9 billion kWh.[4]

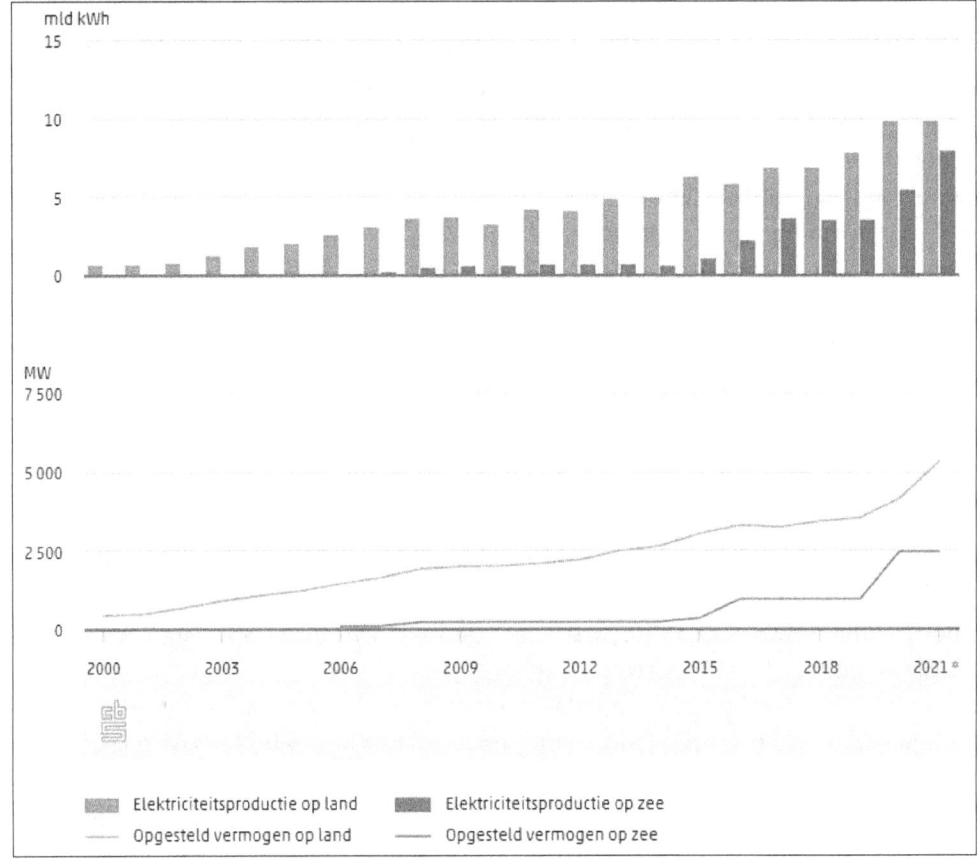

Fig.1.6: The development of installed capacity and the amount of energy generated on land and at sea in the Netherlands.

Figure 1.6 shows the development of installed capacity and the corresponding theoretical amount of energy generated over the last two decades. In recent years there has been an enormous increase in installed capacity and electricity production. The tendency is to invest more in building wind turbines at sea than on land.

Fig. 1.7: The countryside is dominated by wind turbines.

1. www.lowtechmagazine.be/2009/11/geschiedenis-van-de-windmolen.html
2. www.nemokennislink.nl/publicaties/40-jaar-windenergie-in-nederland/
3. www.ge.com/renewableenergy/wind-energy/offshore-wind/haliade-x-offshore-turbine
4. longreads.cbs.nl/netherlands-in-figures-2022/how-many-windmills-stand-in-the-dutch/

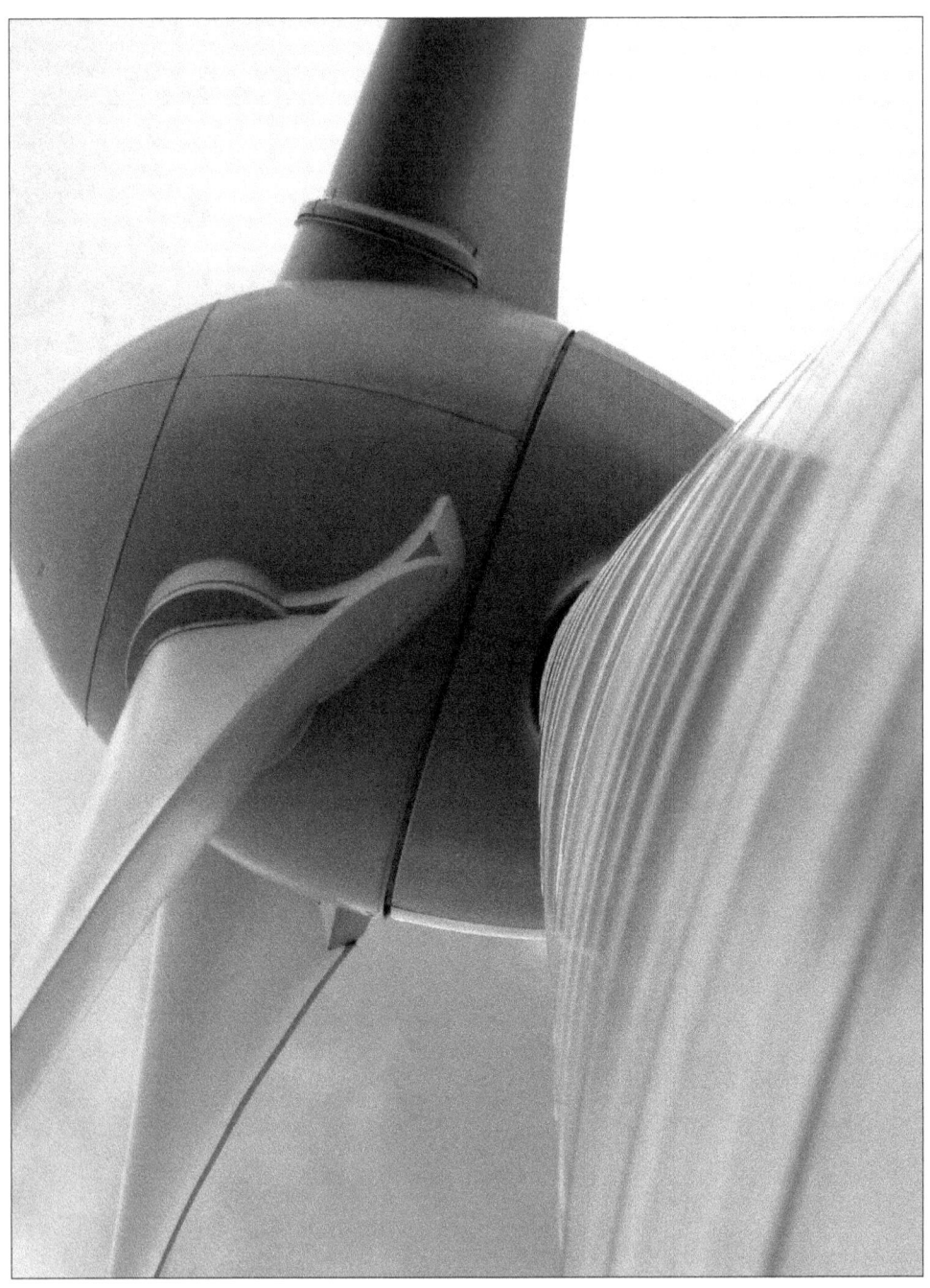

Chapter 2: Wind turbines for generating energy

Wind turbines are designed and built to harvest wind energy. The need for energy in our modern society is huge, which is why many wind turbines are needed to generate enough energy. Burning fossil energy sources such as oil, coal and gas, releases a lot of energy. According to government plans, much of that energy will have to be generated by wind turbines in the future. Many wind turbines spread across the country has a great impact on our living environment, compared to the infrastructure of a limited number of power plants.

As will become clear, wind energy, even with the current number of wind turbines, makes up only a very small part of total energy needs.

This chapter first explains the operating principle of the wind turbine. This will provide tools to understand why wind turbines are getting bigger and bigger. Furthermore, this will provide insight into the natural and technological influences that determine the energy yield of a wind turbine. It is schematically explained how a wind turbine is constructed. This immediately makes clear which materials are needed for construction. The extraction of these - sometimes rare - materials involves numerous environmental aspects. Special attention is given to the ethical aspects, which are often downplayed in the context of energy transition.

The operating principle of the wind turbine

The principle of a wind turbine is simple: the wind makes the blades turn and this movement is converted into electricity - just like a bicycle - with a large dynamo. Behind that simple principle, however, lies a very complex machine.[1] The modern wind turbine uses aerodynamic techniques familiar from the aircraft industry. In addition, the wind industry itself has developed several advanced technologies necessary for efficient operation of the turbine. Those technologies mainly have to do with the fact that wind turbines depend on wind direction and wind speed, even more so than, say, an airplane.

Figure 2.1 shows a cross-section of an aircraft wing where an airflow goes from left to right. [2] The bottom of the wing is straight, and the top is convex. In this way, the air must travel a longer path at

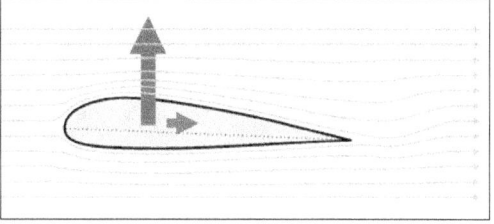

Fig. 2.1: Schematic representation of the cross-section of an aircraft wing where a lift force is generated due to difference in air pressure above and below the wing (green arrow). The red arrow shows the resulting drag force generated by the air.

the top than at the bottom. This creates a difference in air pressure between the top and bottom of the wing, creating an upward force - which we call "suction" or "lift force". This basic aerodynamic principle causes the rotor blades to rotate. To generate the optimum lift force on the rotor blades, the position of the rotor blade relative to the airflow is important. The rotor blade speed is much lower closer to the axis of the wind turbine than at the tip.. After all, that rotor tip has to travel a much greater distance each round. To generate optimal lift force over the entire length of a rotor blade, modern wind turbines exhibit a rotation of the rotor blade from the axis toward the tip of the blade. This rotation is also known as the torsion. With the right torsion in the rotor blade, optimal efficiency can be achieved with respect to lift force - or rotational speed of the rotor.

The lift force, as can be clearly seen in Figure 2.1, is perpendicular to the wind direction. The phenomenon of lift force is also known to roofers throughout the ages. The roof covering is sucked off the roof during storms, not blown. The wing located in the airstream induces a certain resistance that can be expressed in a force. This can be compared to the resistance you experience when cycling against the wind. Spinning rotor blades also induce resistance according to the same principle.

Due to the shape of the rotor blades of a wind turbine, the airflow produces a force in the direction of rotation based on the prevailing aerodynamic principle of an aircraft wing. In the process, the air itself is slowed down. Schematically, this looks like Figure 2.2.[3] The prevailing wind speed is shown as v_0.

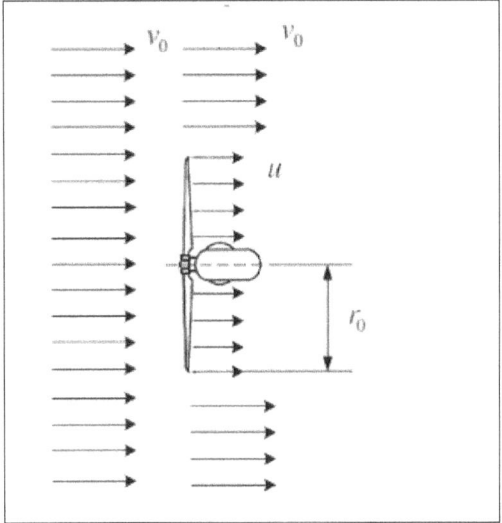

Fig. 2.2: schematic representation of the deceleration of the airflow as it passes the rotor blades of the wind turbine.

When the air has passed the rotor blades of the wind turbine, the speed of the air has decreased - in other words, kinetic energy has been extracted from the air: wind energy has been converted into rotational energy. The speed of the airflow behind the rotor blades is shown as u. If the air is slowed down evenly, the energy generated can be calculated. The greater the difference between the initial speed v_0 and the final speed u, the more energy has been harvested.

A wind turbine positioned directly behind another wind turbine produces less energy when it enters the delayed airflow of the wind turbine in front at a given wind direction. This is the reason why a minimum distance between wind turbines is always maintained, with the average principle being that the distance should be five times the diameter of the rotor.

Wind Power

Wind power generated is proportional to the third power of wind speed. This is the inverse of the power required to move an object through the air at a given speed, such as a car, train, cyclist or airplane. In general, kinetic or kinetic energy of motion is proportional to the square of speed. In the case of wind turbines, to this is added the power generated as a result of the mass of displaced air, which is proportional to the speed times the area encompassed by the rotor blades. The power generated by a wind turbine is therefore proportional to the speed to the power of 3. [4]

The output of a wind turbine depends on its type, wind speed, rated power - that is the maximum power determined by the generator, the time a wind turbine can run and the efficiency of converting wind energy to electricity. The term "full-load hours" is used to express the output of a wind turbine. If a wind turbine delivers its rated output, then each hour is exactly one full-load hour. If a turbine delivers half of its rated power in light winds, then each hour is half a full-load hour.

Thus, since the area covered by the rotor blades helps determine the energy output of a wind turbine and this area forms a circle (see Figure 2.3), the energy output is proportional to the square of the rotor diameter. For example, if the rotor diameter increases 2x, the power output increases by a factor of 4. This is why larger and larger wind turbines are made.

There is, however, a natural limit to the amount of energy a wind turbine can extract from the air. If all energy were extracted from the air, the air would come to a standstill after passing through the rotor blades, blocking the supply of new air. According to Betz's law - developed by Albert Betz[5] - there is a theoretical maximum amount of energy that can be extracted from flowing air by means of a rotor - for example, the rotor blades of a wind turbine. After theoretical considerations, he concluded that there is a factor - the performance coefficient - that indicates the maximum amount of energy a wind turbine can extract from the airstream. This factor, denoted Cp, is found to be theoretically at most 0.593. The modern rotor has a Cp value of about 0.4 to 0.5, which corresponds to about 70 to 80% of what is theoretically possible. The theoretically maximum Cp value is not achieved, mainly due to energy losses in the rotor. In addition,

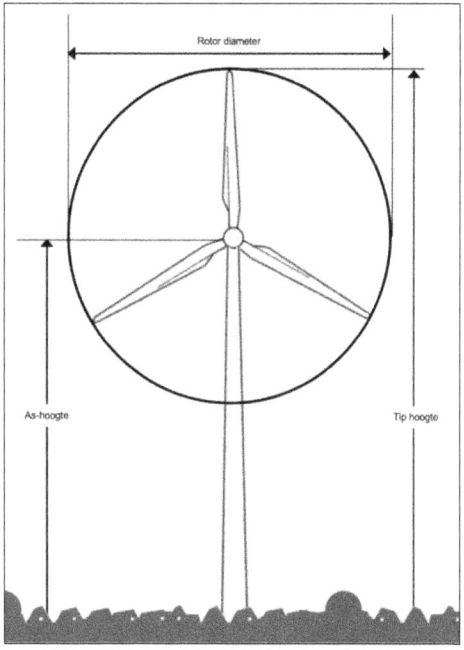

Fig. 2.3: The shaft height, tip height and rotor diameter of a wind turbine. The circle forms the covered area of the rotor blades.

the practically achievable maximum Cp value of the modern rotor is achieved only when the wind blows at a speed of between 6 - 11 meters per second; that is wind force 4 to 6 Beaufort. If the wind force is lower or higher, the performance coefficient Cp becomes lower quite quickly.

Wind turbines with 3 rotor blades, with a diameter of 60 m and a shaft height of 70 m, can deliver about 1 to 1.5 megawatts (MW) of power at an optimal wind speed - wind force 6. A larger wind turbine with a rotor diameter of 130 m and a shaft height of 90 m can achieve a power output of 3.8 megawatts (MW).

However, there are some limitations as far as efficiency is concerned with ever-increasing rotor diameters. With very large rotor diameters, efficiency does not decrease, but the wind turbine must be designed for a lower speed. This is because the speed of the ends of the rotor blades must not exceed about 75 m/s, or 270 km/h, at most. Indeed, above that, the rotor noise produced becomes a problem.

During the period 1980-2023, the "standard" wind turbine has become progressively larger. The rotor diameter of a wind turbine depends on the generator power, the shaft height, and the local wind regime. On the coast, it blows a bit harder at 100 m than inland. As a result, wind turbines further away from the coast have higher towers and/or longer rotor blades.

The structure of the wind turbine

Most modern wind turbines have three rotor blades. The point where the blades come together is called the rotor. So the wind causes the whole thing to rotate. As mentioned, it follows from aerodynamic principles that resistance is created in addition to lift force. Research has shown that the more rotor blades a wind turbine has, the more drag it experiences. This means that the wind turbine cannot spin as fast, which also means that less energy can be generated. The advantage is that a wind turbine with more rotor blades makes less noise. An optimum must be found between yield and noise for each location. Because of this, wind turbines on land usually have 3 rotor blades and wind turbines at sea are often used with 2 rotor blades. This also obviously saves costs because less material is needed, but it does create additional noise. The latter, as we will see later, plays into environmental pollution of people and animals.

The rotor in turn is coupled to a nacelle. This is the housing at the top of the pylon. A special motor - "yaw motor" - also ensures that the nacelle is always positioned so that the blades face the wind. This is important for maximum efficiency. To determine the correct direction of the nacelle, a wind vane on top of the wind turbine continuously measures the wind direction.

Inside the nacelle there is a generator: a large dynamo - a giant bicycle dynamo - which converts the rotating motion of the rotor into electricity. This involves the use of magnets, which can be used in various ways. For a wind turbine, the best choice is

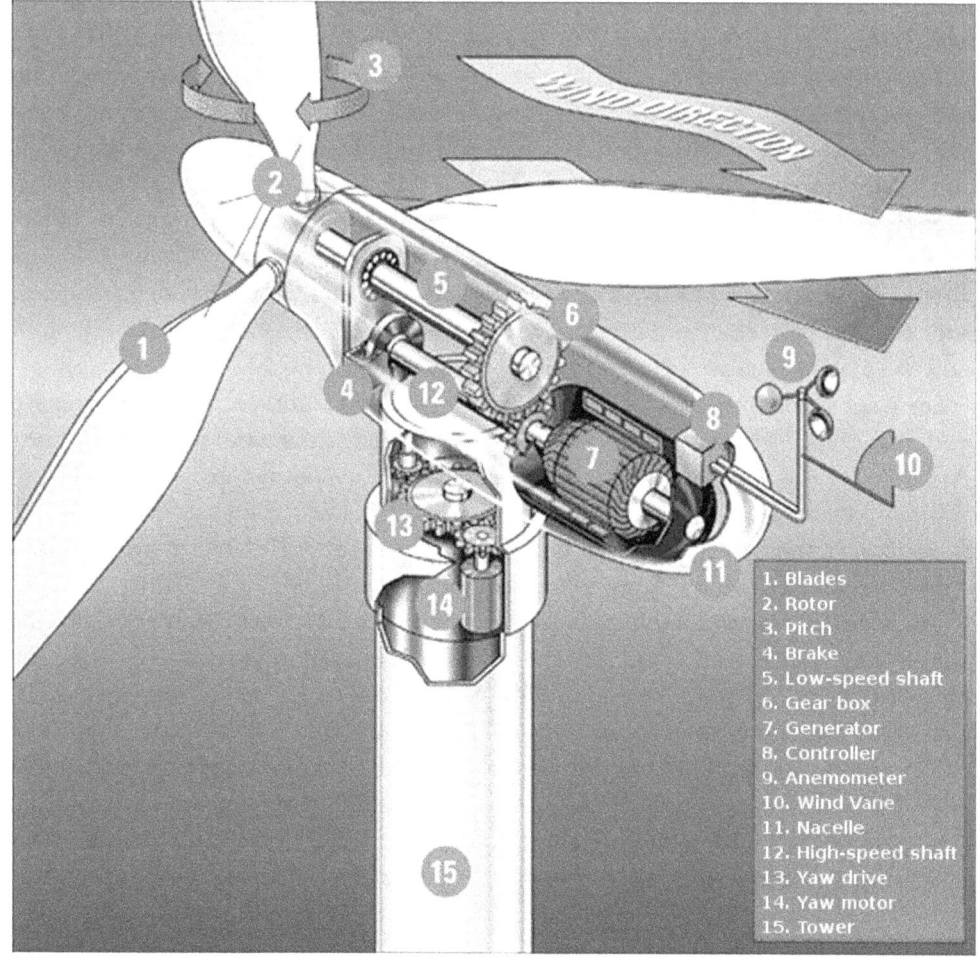

Fig. 2.4: The main components of the wind turbine.[6]

an alternator that operates at low speed. The permanent magnet alternator best meets these requirements. It is also the most used alternator in well-designed wind turbines. Wind power plant turbines in Delfzijl use the "direct drive" principle, which means that the generator is driven directly by the rotor. The rotational speed of the generator shaft and rotor shaft are then equal.

In other turbines, the generator is driven via a vertical shaft and gearbox, which ensures that the relatively low rotational speed of the rotor is converted to the higher rotational speed required by the generator in this turbine to generate electricity. The generator is then again connected to a transformer, which converts the low voltage obtained by the generator into high voltage.

In recent years, permanent magnet generator (PMG) systems in wind turbines have eliminated the need for gearboxes. This has resulted in more cost-effective, reliable operation, reduced maintenance, and improved grid compatibility. Magnets allow the removal of mechanical gearboxes. This helps meet the operational and economic challenges of modern wind turbines. The magnetic field of neodymium magnets does not require an external power source. Therefore, fewer parts are needed than in older systems, which require additional maintenance.

The generators in wind turbines require very strong permanent magnets. Rare materials are used in neodymium magnets. Made of neodymium, iron and boron, these magnets are the strongest permanent magnets available economically. They are already being used in some of the largest wind turbines in the world. Neodymium magnets provide efficient electricity generation. That lowers costs, improves reliability, and reduces costly maintenance. [7]

The higher above the earth's surface, the stronger the wind. Therefore, wind turbines should preferably be placed as high as possible. The higher the rotor, the more wind the blades can catch and the more energy they can generate.

Since subsidies were awarded in 2015 within the Stimulation of Sustainable Energy Production (SDE+) based on the average wind speed at the wind turbine location, a wind map for the Netherlands at 100 meters height was drawn by the KNMI based on the model called HARMONIE. Figure 2.5 shows the actual measurement data for the town of Cabauw compared to the model developed by KNMI. It shows the differences in wind speed at 10 meters and higher altitudes. [8]

Advances in the wind industry have ensured that a 50-meter pylon has long since ceased to be considered "high. Wind turbines in the Netherlands have now reached shaft heights of up to 135 meters, with even an outlier of up to 150 meters. The Zeewolde Wind Farm, which opened in 2022, now has wind turbines with a tip height of 220 meters, and the limit has not yet been reached. Danish wind turbine manufacturer Vestas, in cooperation with the company Max Bögl, has designed a wind turbine with a shaft height of 199 meters and a tip height of 285 meters. It would currently be the tallest turbine on land in the world. Installations of these wind turbines are planned for 2025 in Germany and Austria. The size of the rotor blades has also increased over the past 10 years from about 40 meters to 80 meters. This means that today the rotor diameter can be as much as 160 meters. In November 2022, the company LM Wind Power even managed to certify rotor blades up to 107 meters in length.[9][10][11] This paves the way for large-scale application of these huge rotor blades.

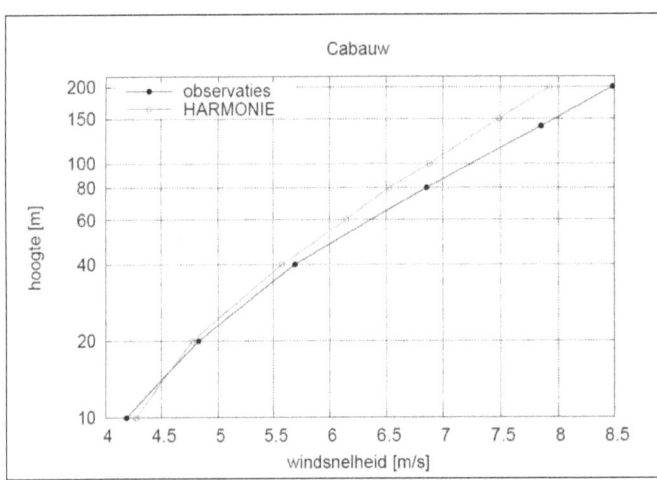

Fig. 2.5: Wind speed in m/s at different altitudes according to observations and according to the KNMI model (HARMONIE). The model overestimated the exchange of kin energy from the air to the lower air layers. This explains the difference between the model and observations.

The higher the wind turbine, the larger and stronger the pylon must be. At the base, the pylon diameter of the average wind turbine is 4 to 6 meters. With increasing height, the pylon can be as much as about 10 meters in diameter. There are even plans to build 20 MW wind turbines with a pylon diameter of 12 meters. Inside the wind turbine there is also a computer that is connected to external computers by GSM, cables, or satellite dish. This allows remote control and monitoring of the turbine. The live data you can follow via the app is also provided by these computers.

Wind turbines begin to generate electricity at a wind speed of 3 to 4 meters per second (3 Beaufort), the so-called cut-in wind speed. Once the wind increases further, the wind turbine produces more and more electricity until the maximum power output of the wind turbine is reached. This happens at a wind speed of about 12 meters per second, which corresponds to about 6 Beaufort. If the wind blows harder, the rotor must be slowed down or, in extreme winds, the rotor must even be stopped to prevent damage to the wind turbine due to the enormous forces that then act on the structure. It is not the case that a wind turbine generates more and more electricity in strong or stormy winds, simply because the generator cannot handle it.

Today, the rotor blades of wind turbines are automatically turned to the wind by electronics. Those same electronics also cause the rotor blades to be turned out of the wind when the wind gets too strong. This is necessary because in high winds, the

Fig. 2.6: A view inside the pylon of a wind turbine with ladder and cables. The diameter of the mast can be as much as 10 meter.

stress concentrations in the blades can exceed the critical limit of the material due to the high loads. This can cause the rotor blades to break off. The fact that wind turbines not only generate electricity but also use electricity is often forgotten. Multiple wind turbine components use electricity, such as blade angle adjustment, lights, controllers, communications, sensors, data collection, oil heater, pump, cooler, filtration system in gear boxes and many more. Data on electricity consumption of wind turbines is difficult to ascertain, but because of all these electronically controlled components, small wind turbines may consume more electricity than they generate. On Feb. 5, 2023, the Scottish Sunday Mail newspaper reported that in December 2022, 71 wind turbines at the Arecleoch Wind and Glenn App wind farms had to be kept warm with diesel generators to keep them ice-free. [12]

The rotor blades

In the past, wind turbine blades were manufactured from wood. Technological developments and ever-increasing requirements have led to the application of composites in rotor blades of a modern wind turbine. A composite is a material consisting of several components. For rotor blades, the use of fiberglass reinforced epoxy combined with balsa wood has emerged as the best alternative. This material is also suitable for the ever-increasing size of wind turbines and rotor blades. The composite blades meet strength and stiffness requirements, offer a high degree of freedom of shape, are cost-effective and have a low specific gravity, making them ideally suited for this application.

The main raw materials to produce the required glass fibers are quartz sand, clay with a high content of aluminum oxide and limestone. The raw materials are mixed in the right proportions and then melted into liquid glass in a furnace at a temperature of 1400°C. Pulling the liquid glass at several hundred km/h creates gossamer threads of glass that can be spun.

Balsa wood is the lightest type of wood commonly available. Its density ranges from 40 to 300 kg/m^3 at 12% moisture content. The most common density of 150 kg/m^3 is used in rotor blades. The wood comes from a fast-growing tree from Central and South America, which in its natural habitat can reach a height of over 20 meters in five years and a diameter of 0.7 to 1.2 meters.

Epoxy is a synthetic resin that uses two chemical components - usually diglycidyl ethers and a combination of bisphenol A and epichlorohydrin - to cure. Epoxy resins come in different hardnesses and color compositions. At elevated temperature, the components react with each other. Under pressure - usually a vacuum - they are then cured to their final shape-solid state. Epoxy resins are highly resistant to elevated temperatures and chemicals, making them ideal for numerous industrial applications. Epoxy resins are thermosetting plastics, which means that once cured, they cannot be remelted, something that is possible with thermoplastics. Thermosetting plastics can therefore only be disposed of at the end of their life by combustion. In the process, the plastic reacts with oxygen, releasing numerous toxic gases in addition to CO_2 and water.

The foundation of wind turbines

Both onshore and offshore wind turbines need solid foundations. That foundation must absorb the forces transmitted down through the pylon by the wind. The higher the pylon and the higher the wind load, the greater the bending moment that must be absorbed by the foundation. Due to the varying nature of the wind and wind direction, varying loads also occur. We also call this a "fatigue load". These varying loads in themselves are not high enough to cause direct visible damage to the wind turbine, but they can cause small cracks in the construction. This problem is known from aerospace engineering but will not be further elaborated here.

The soil conditions of the location where the wind turbine is to be installed determine the foundation required.

Before building a wind turbine on land can begin, several preparations are needed. First, all tower components such as nacelle, hub and rotor blades must be transported from all parts of the world, often by special transports, to the tower site or wind farm. Transportation takes place via (high-speed) roads and inland waterways, and if necessary, by sea.

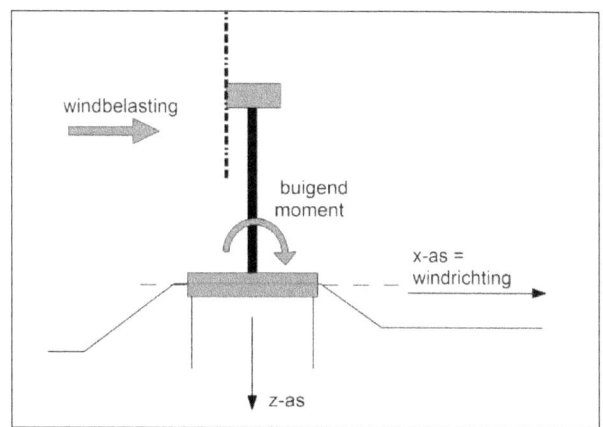

Fig. 2.7: Schematic representation of the bending moment on the foundation of a wind turbine due to the wind load.

For concrete trucks, cranes and other traffic to get to the construction site safely, proper (temporary) construction roads are needed. Those construction roads will be built from the nearest paved roads. Around the area where the turbine will be located, a large part of the site will be paved with rubble. This is necessary to support the heavy trucks bringing in materials and to provide enough room to maneuver.

After completion of construction roads and crane sidings, piles are usually driven for foundations. In the Noordoostpolder wind farm, for example, which opened in 2017, 26 wind turbines were installed on land at that time. A total of 45 kilometers of concrete piles were needed for the foundation of all these wind turbines of the Enercon E-26 type. Each wind turbine with a tip height of 198 meters involved 66 piles of 23 to 30 meters in length and a diameter of 50 by 50 cm. Between one thousand and two thousand strokes were needed to drive such a pile into the former Zuiderzee soil. This hammering is usually done using diesel equipment.

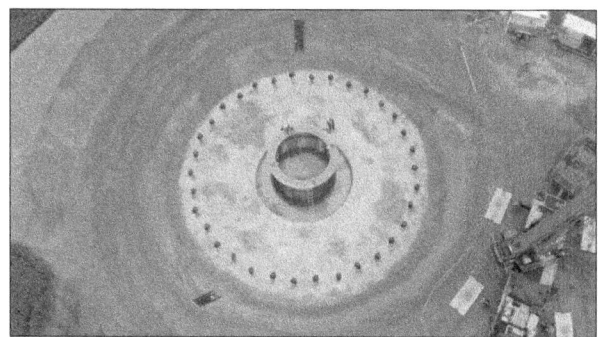

Fig. 2.8: Construction pit and foundation of a wind turbine with 34 piles.[15]

On the piles will be a block of concrete 26 meters in diameter, with a thickness of as much as 4 meters. In this example, the individual pile had a total weight of 16,000 kg. Of that, 765 kg is rebar, the rest is concrete. The wind turbine weighs a total of 2,800,000 kg and the foundation 2,500,000 kg. [13][14]

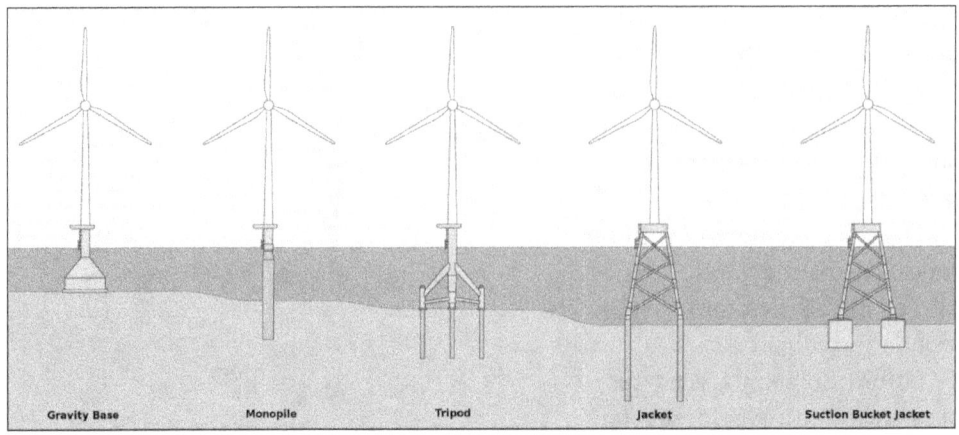
Fig. 2.9: Types of foundations for offshore wind turbines.

At sea, there are very different issues when placing wind turbines. Depending on the local depth of the sea and the condition of the seabed, different types of foundations for offshore wind turbines are possible. Gravity-based foundations can be used at depths between 0 and 30 meters. These foundations consist of large blocks of steel or concrete resting on the seabed. A second type of foundation consists of a steel cylinder - the "suction-bucket" - on which a shaft is mounted. These are installed by the pressure differential between the inside of the bucket and the surrounding water. The best known and most widely used monopile (one-pile) foundations are installed in shallow water (between 0 and 30 meters deep) - as, for example, in the North Sea - and consist of a pile that is forced into the seabed. The cost of these monopiles is relatively low which makes them popular. The tripods are used at depths from 20 to 80 meters. They consist of 3 legs connected to a central shaft that forms the base of the wind turbine. Each leg stands on a pile that is forced into the seabed. Such a wide foundation makes it applicable for wind turbines placed in areas with greater sea depths. Finally, so-called jacket foundations are used. These are lattice structures that allow placement in areas with depths between 20 and 80 meters. The truss construction is placed on three or four piles. These piles are also forced into the seabed.

Piling in the seabed

The driving of the piles for the structures causes incredible noise under water. Even after taking various measures such as air shields, a slow start to the piling and the application of sound-absorbing structures, the noise travels in shock waves far through the water. For a monopile foundation, the pile driving time is a maximum of 2 hours. However, when using tripod or jacket foundations, the total pile driving time increases because multiple piles are driven per foundation, 3 for a tripod or 4 for a jacket foundation, respectively. The total pile driving time per foundation is approximately 3 to 4.5 hours for tripods and 4 to 6 hours for jackets.[16] Thus, the pile driving time is quite limited. However, it should be borne in mind that a wind farm will soon comprise about 100 wind turbines, so a lot of piles have to be driven. Because sound propagates faster and farther in water, a large area is thus constantly exposed to noise. The impact of noise on marine life is described later in Chapter 6.

The foundations are largely produced from steel. Consequently, a jacket foundation weighs as much as more than 500,000 kg. Often overlooked is the amount of energy required to produce, transport, and install such structures. A whole arsenal of very large lifting equipment has been designed and produced specifically to install and maintain wind turbines at sea. These resources also draw on our Earth's materials supply. The energy for producing and placing them comes mainly from fossil fuels.

Figure 2.10 illustrates the sheer size of such structures, which must be transported by ships to the construction site. Ships also still mostly run on fuel oil and diesel.

Once the piles for offshore wind turbines are in place, it often takes some time before the rotor can be placed on the pile. To protect the cabling already in the pile and the inside of the pile itself from dirt and corrosion from the salty marine environment, the piles are temporarily sealed at the top with a cover cap. These caps are usually made of steel (or aluminum) and are used only once. All in all, therefore, much, much steel is needed to build wind turbines. So let's also look at where those materials come from.

Fig. 2.10: Tripod and jacket foundations at Cuxhaven in Germany, ready for transport.

Raw materials and mining

The production of a wind turbine requires a variety of raw materials. These include a large amount of concrete for the foundation and a huge amount of steel mainly for the pylon. In addition, the rotor blades are manufactured from fiberglass reinforced thermoset plastics. Figure 2.11 shows that 220 tons of coal must be extracted per MW of rated power of a wind turbine to produce the required amount of steel. That is the same amount needed to produce 220 small cars.

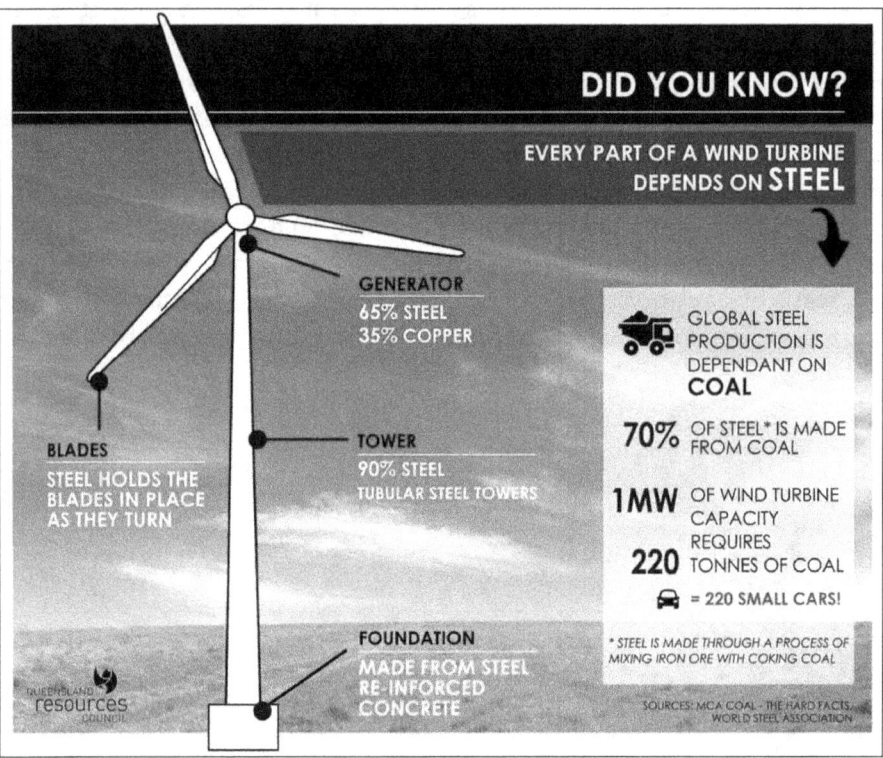

Fig. 2.11: An impression of the amount of steel - and hence coal - required to build a wind turbine.

Producing a unit of renewable energy requires a much higher investment than producing that same unit of energy with fossil fuels.[17]

One wind turbine with a rated capacity of 4 MW requires approximately 900,000 kg of steel, 2,500,000 kg of concrete and 45,000 kg of fiber reinforced plastic. [18]

In 2018, 84.5% of global energy consumption was based on fossil fuels. The plan to completely replace fossil fuels with renewable energy by 2050 has only recently led to solid research. The question here was whether there are enough minerals available to meet this goal. The production of the required solar panels, wind turbines and batteries, among other things, requires huge amounts of minerals. Simon Michaux, working at GTK (Geological Survey of Finland) was able to find out what the global electricity consumption was in 2018 through extensive research. Based on that, he has mapped out the Agenda 2030 and 2050 goals, in terms of phasing out fossil fuels, in terms of the minerals needed.

By minerals, think of common metals such as steel and copper, but also cobalt, manganese and various other rare minerals needed to produce batteries, solar panels and wind turbines. His outstanding research was published in 2022. Scientists working for the government have been unable to provide grounded commentary on his work a year later. What emerges is that current mines and anticipated reserves in yet-to-be mined areas of Earth are nowhere near sufficient to supply the required quantities of minerals. In doing so, his study assumes an amount of electricity that should be available for a generation. This does not include replacement of wind turbines and solar farms at the end of their useful life - about 20 years.

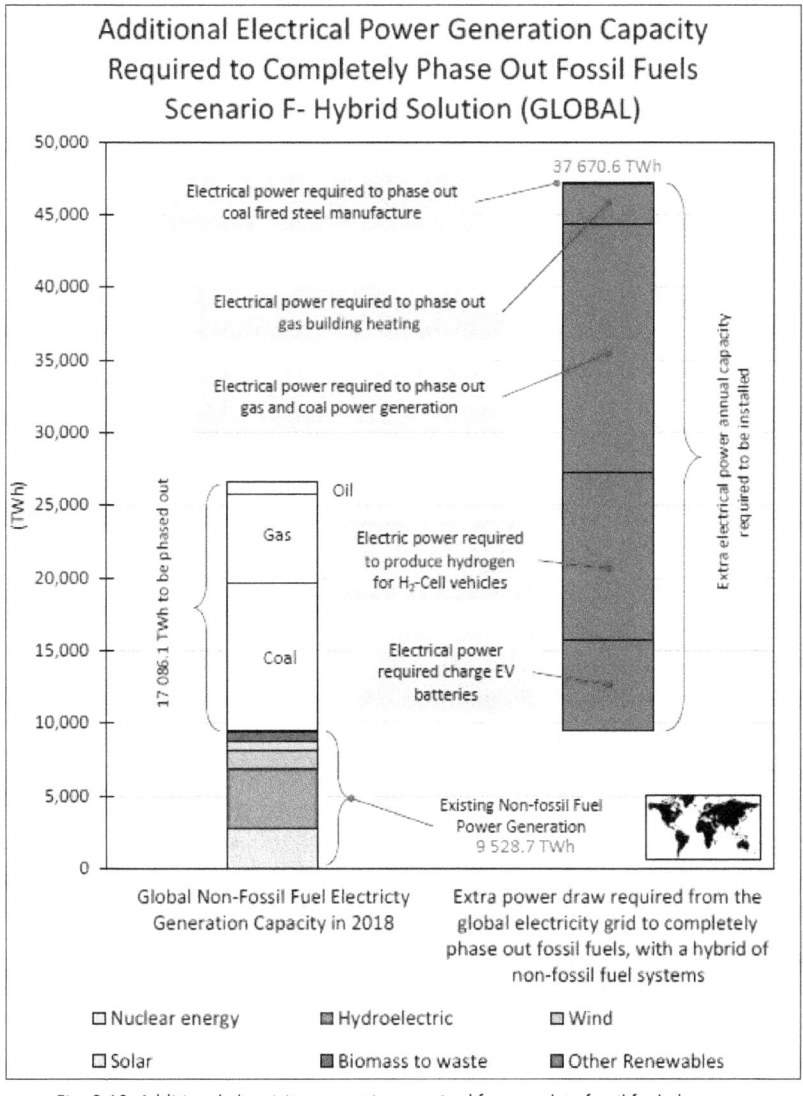

Fig. 2.12: Additional electricity generation required for complete fossil fuel phase-out.

Figure 2.12 (next page) shows the amount of additional electricity that would need to be generated annually if fossil fuels were fully phased out. This is based on global electricity production in 2018, two years before the corona crisis. A comparison with subsequent years would give an unfair and distorted picture. Current electricity production is back to its former 2018 level and the trend is upward. In 2018, total electricity production in the world was 26.614 TWh.

Economic growth and the related increasing demand for energy is not included in this picture and as mentioned earlier, this still does not include the replacement of the numerous batteries, solar farms, and wind turbines. So, this is an extremely lean scenario.

In areas where winters are cold and dark, and there is little wind, not enough electricity will be produced in the future, when it is precisely during this period that the need for energy is highest. Under such conditions, energy must be stored in batteries. Figure 2.13 gives an impression of such a power plant. This is the Hornsdale power station in Australia, the largest battery in the world with a storage capacity of 100 MW/129 MWh - now expanded by 50 MW. [19]

Fig. 2.13: Hornsdale Power Station in Australia.

To have sufficient electricity available during cold, dark and windless periods, a total of over 15.000.000 Hornsdale power stations will be needed worldwide by the year 2050, according to Michaux.

These will then have a combined storage capacity of 548.9 TWh which should be sufficient for a 4-week electricity buffer. The calculation was made based on the target installed capacity generated by both solar farms and wind farms. Tesla batteries at the Hornsdale power station have a guaranteed life of 15 years and will need to be replaced in the not-too-distant future. [20][21]

Michaux's work is broken down into several parts, of which energy to be generated by wind turbines is only one. The United Nations has included in its 2050 goals a percentage as wind energy's share of the world's total energy needs. This was then divided into a portion of wind energy on land and a portion at sea with a land/sea split of 70/30. Assuming the need for energy in 2050 and the intended share of wind energy in it, it was calculated that about 1.5 million wind turbines on land and 630 thousand at sea are needed. This number is in addition to the already existing wind turbines. This calculation assumes a capacity per wind turbine of 3MW. So, the total additional capacity required, compared to today, is just under 14.000 TWh.

Figure 2.14 shows how many kg of minerals are required to produce 1MW of rated power.[22] This gives a clear picture of the huge amounts of minerals required to achieve the phase-out of fossil fuels.

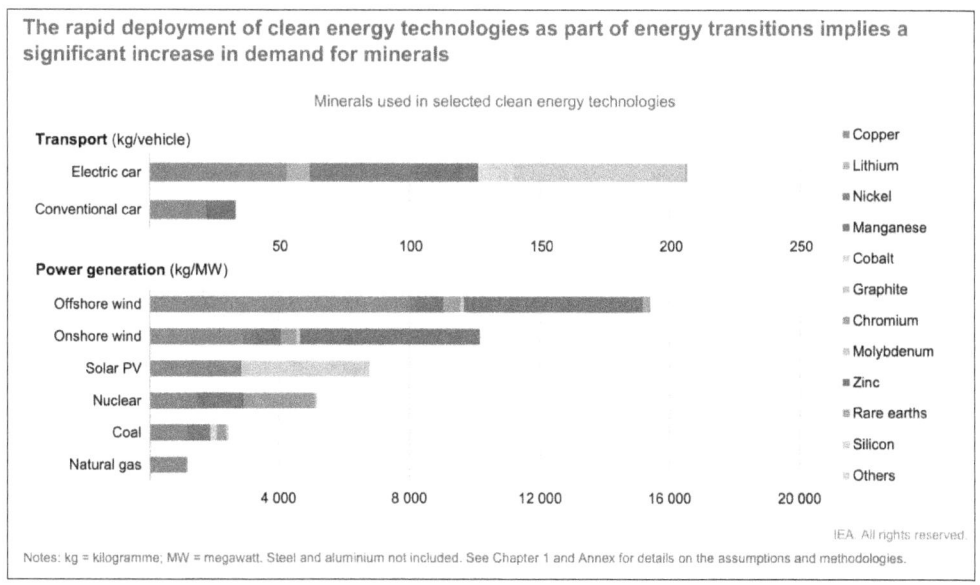

Fig. 2.14: Amount of minerals - in kilograms - required to generate 1 MW of nominal power.
This overview excludes steel and aluminum.

Figures from United States Geological Survey (USGS) show which and how many minerals are needed to produce enough electricity for a generation. In addition, an overview of global reserves. When the reserves are expressed as percentages of the total amount of resources needed, it appears that there is an ample shortage of the following minerals: Copper, Nickel, Lithium, Cobalt, Graphite and Vandium. In the case of Lithium, there is currently a 98% shortfall to meet the 2050 fossil fuel phase-out targets.

So new mines would have to be explored for the needed minerals. However, this is not so easy. Out of every thousand sites where minerals have been found in the ground, only two can eventually be economically exploited. There is a 20-year time limit for the economic exploitation of a mine. Even then, mines do not in all cases turn out to break even, so they must be closed. That fate befalls twenty to thirty percent of mines. Currently, when a site with a large amount of rare earths is found, such as in Sweden in January 2023, only euphoric reports appear in the media regarding the energy transition. However, all the above facts are then ignored. A discovery does not yet immediately lead to the extraction of these minerals. [23]

Cobalt

Cobalt is used in a whole range of industrial processes. However, its use in battery electrodes is currently one of the most important applications of cobalt. Seventy percent of the world's cobalt production takes place in the African Democratic Republic of Congo. The cobalt mining industry in Congo consists of legal mines and illegal mines, and much controversial child labor takes place. That Congolese children put

Fig. 2.15: Child labour in mines in Congo. (Julien Harneis: Wikimedia Commons)

their lives on the line for the batteries in our I-phones and electric cars is known to few consumers.

While it is suggested that electric driving would be sustainable, no one mentions that big companies like Tesla use cobalt and pay no attention to how it is extracted from the ground in Congo. Car giant Tesla has even bought into the company Glencore, accused of corruption. The partnership between Glencore and Israeli businessman Dan Gertler is highly problematic when it comes to corruption. Gertler got his hands on mining concessions in Congo through his friendship with former President Kabilla. He resold those rights to Glencore. Criminal investigations are now underway against him and in the U.S., he is on a sanctions list (U.S. Department of State Executive Order 13818).

The Netherlands also plays a dubious role in this case. After all, Gertler's company is based in the Netherlands and takes advantage of the Dutch tax climate. Despite questions being asked by members of Parliament about Gertler and possible corruption, nothing has changed yet. The Dutch government is guilty of, to say the least, questionable practices in Congo. Three countries are under criminal investigation for corruption at the company. Nevertheless, Glencore can continue to operate as usual and the Dutch pension fund ABP invests fully in Glencore.[24] (Glencore International AG is an international trading house based in Baar, Switzerland. The company trades metals, minerals, energy and agricultural products and is also actively involved in their production. The company was founded in 1974 and has been publicly traded since May 18, 2011).

Lithium

Although not required for wind turbine production, lithium mining is indirectly related to it. After all, some of the energy generated by wind turbines will have to be stored in large batteries in the future, to have a buffer of energy when the energy demand exceeds the instantaneous amount of energy generated.

Chile, the world's second-largest producer of lithium with a 20 percent market share, is all about lithium. Chile holds half the world's reserves of lithium, and Chilean lithium can be extracted at low cost. Lithium is what the energy transition is all about. The metal is essential for constructing batteries for electric vehicles and, in fact, anything with a battery. However, lithium resources are not infinite, as mentioned earlier. The environmental impact of its extraction has hardly been studied yet. What is already clear is that the environmental impact is heavy.

But lithium mining is not just about the environment. Culture also suffers. The numerous mines installed near villages and towns have already caused major health problems and social change in Chile. The Atacama Salar in Chile is the driest salt desert in the world. Lithium production is in full swing there. The salt flat of Atacama is a sacred place belonging to the ancestral history of the Chilean people. Hidden beneath the salt flats is coveted lithium. The area was once flooded with water. That water evaporated and formed salt basins called "salars." Lithium has been mined here since the 1980s.

Fig. 2.16: Lithium baths in Chile.

Miners pump brine, containing lithium, from a massive reservoir beneath the Atacama salt flats to huge pools on the surface of the desert. The liquid is moved from pool to pool, and after a long solar bath lasting twelve to eighteen months, the coveted mineral is finally obtained in the form of lithium chloride. It is then transported 270 kilometers to the lithium carbonate and hydroxide plants. It reacts with another material, sodium chloride, which is imported by ship from other countries. During the evaporation process, up to 95 percent of the water from the extracted brine evaporates. This accelerates water scarcity in the Atacama, with all its consequences for the natural habitat. The nearly 5-kilometer-long baths, the largest of which covers 280 thousand square meters, require very large amounts of water.

In 2020, Chile's environmental court required mining company Soquimich (SQM) to set up a permanent online monitoring system on pollution of surrounding freshwater. However, there appeared to be many errors in the system. For example, one of the lagoons next to a freshwater catchment area is not monitored.

However, most scientists agree that the Atacama salt flats are a very fragile ecosystem, where everything is interconnected. The salt flats that include flamingos, Vicunas and lizards are being devastated by lithium mining.

Faced with this problem, one of SQM's goals is to reduce the use of pumped brine by 65%. The credibility of this goal is questionable since the company has been owned by the nephew of the former Chilean general since the Pinochet dictatorship. This owner has faced cases of hidden financing of political campaigns, convictions for environmental pollution and failure to respect the rights of indigenous peoples.

In addition to the ecological disaster, the mining companies cause deep conflicts in the communities. In the indigenous villages, some work with the mine or accept the money, others refuse to cooperate, leading to much tension in these communities, which traditionally function as one big family. [25]

Fig. 2.17: A picture of a poison lake in Baotou due to the increased production of Neodymium.

The mining of rare minerals also raises question marks in China. The British Daily Mail newspaper caused a stir back in 2011 with a report on the Chinese industrial city of Baotou, the site of much of the world's neodymium mining. The report included shocking photos of toxic lakes and stories from residents about health problems such as cancer, skin and dental problems.

Neodymium is very difficult to extract. It is not, like copper, concentrated in a "vein" in the ground, but is mixed with other substances. In Baotou, for example, the neodymium must be separated from uranium and thorium, two radioactive materials. Those substances, along with other toxic chemicals, are dumped into lakes and basins with little or no protection after the neodymium is extracted. The groundwater is thus contaminated with radioactive material. The air there also contains high concentrations of toxic substances, making plants, animals and people fatally ill.

China is one of the largest suppliers of minerals. Not because these substances can only be found in China, but mainly because it is one of the few countries that dares to do the dirty, toxic and often radioactive work that the rest of the world has long shunned. China's failure to take measures to curb environmental pollution does not mean that clean extraction of neodymium is impossible. Products are only truly clean if they are made with respect for people and the environment from start to finish. For the wind industry, this, what environmental experts call "chain consciousness," will be crucial to maintaining the "clean energy source" qualification. [26][27][28][29]

The examples of mineral extraction in Congo, Chile and China illustrate how the United Nations' goals work out in practice for the landscape, large ecosystems, and society as a whole. The fact that the lack of diverse minerals needed for the energy transition is not recognized as such by world political leaders shows a serious lack of knowledge, depth, and realism. Corrupt corporations cause devastations to ultimately make a small (and perhaps negative) contribution to goals that are already intrinsically unachievable in practice.

1. www.windcentrale.nl/blog/hoe-werkt-een-windmolen/
2. wikikids.com/Flying
3. www.natuurkunde.nl/artikelen/3329/de-hoogste-dynamos-ter-wereld
4. en.wikipedia.org/wiki/Wind_power
5. en.wikipedia.org/wiki/Betz%27s_law
6. www.energyrefuge.com/
7. www.amazingmagnets.com
8. Technical Report; TR-351, Wind map of the Netherlands at 100 meters altitude, KNMI 2014
9. windpowernl.com
10. www.nwea.nl
11. www.vestas.com
12. www.dailyrecord.co.uk/news/scottish-news/dozens-scottish-power-wind-turbines-29135763
13. handbook-precast-concrete.betonhuis.nl/
14. www.windparknoordoostpolder.nl
15. drentsemondenoostermoer.nl/de-construction-of-a-wind-turbine/
16. EIA Offshore wind energy area Borssele. Effects of construction of lots III and IV on marine mammals, Dr. F.Heinis, Final Report dated September 2, 2015; www.rvo.nl/sites/default/files/2015%2011%2024%20MER%20kavel%20III%20[GM-0172781]_Def_Depart3%20-%20Annexes%203%20tm%2015.pdf
17. Global Energy Observatory, Agora Energiewende and Sandbag 2019
18. www.drentsemondenooster-moer.nl; Enercon-26
19. hornsdalepowerreserve.com.au/
20. GTK Open File Work Report 42/2021; Assessment of the Additional Capacity Required of Alternative Energy Electrical Power Systems to Completely Replace Fossil Fuels; Simon P. Michaux

Fig. 2.18: The invisible structural components of offshore wind turbines are unimaginably large.

21 (126) Assoc Prof Simon Michaux - The quantity of metals required to manufacture just one generation of... - YouTube

22. (PDF) The Role of Critical Minerals in Clean Energy Transitions (IEA); iea.blob.core.windows.net/assets/ffd2a83b-8c30-4e9d-980a-52b6d9a86fdc/TheRoleofCriticalMineralsinCleanEnergyTransitions.pdf

23. lkab.com/en/press/europes-largest-deposit-of-rare-earth-metals-is-located-in-the-kiruna-area/

24. kro-ncrv.co.uk/children-in-congo-car-their-lives-for-a-tesla-battery

25. europeantimes.news/2021/11/in-chile-everything-for-lithium-at-the-expense-of-the-environment

26. www.dailymail.co.uk/home/moslive/article-1350811/In-China-true-cost-Britains-clean-green-wind-power-experiment-Pollution-disastrous-scale.html

27. www.bloomberg.com/news/articles/2011-01-05/china-rare-earths-leave-toxic-trail-to-toyota-prius-vestas-wind-turbines#xj4y7vzkg

28. daserste.ndr.de/panorama/archiv/2011/Das-schmutzige-Geheimnis-sauberer-Windraeder,windkraft189.html

29. www.nytimes.com/2010/10/30/business/global/30rare.html?pagewanted=all

Chapter 3: Climate policy and the implications for society

In our modern society, almost everything we do requires energy. The most reliable and economical way for generating energy is through gas and coal-fired power plants. Current global climate policy, initiated in 1992, means that this reliable and inexpensive way of generating energy will have to be largely replaced by solar and wind generated energy. Nuclear power is a separate topic - with both fierce proponents and opponents - regardless of whether nuclear power will become part of the energy transition I leave it out of consideration here.

Even though climate policy is global, in practice it means that there will be direct and profound impacts on countries, regions, cities and villages. In other words, smaller and smaller communities and ultimately for each person individually. In this book, we focus on wind energy. From abstract global policy to concrete questions such as: why should there be wind turbines in my community? How many wind turbines will soon be behind my house and what will the consequences be? To answer these questions, it is necessary to first understand how climate goals have been established at the global level.

The first global agreements on environment and development were established in 1992 in United Nations Agenda 21. This agenda was followed up in 2015, with agreements set forth in Agenda 2030. Both agendas led to European laws and regulations that are eventually translated into national and then regional policies. Concrete examples will illustrate how such policies work out in practice.

Agenda 21

Agenda 21 is a 21st century-oriented, comprehensive action plan to be implemented globally, nationally and locally by United Nations agencies and governments, in every area where humans impact the environment.[1] Agenda 21, the Rio Declaration on Environment and Development and the Declaration of Principles for Sustainable Forest Management, was adopted by 179 countries at the United Nations Conference on Environment and Development - UNCED - in Rio de Janeiro, Brazil, June 3 to 14, 1992. The Rio Declaration is also known as the Earth Summit. At this Earth Summit, global policies that should lead to the replacement of fossil fuels for energy generation emerged for the first time. In fact, fossil fuels are directly linked to climate change.

Subsequently, the Commission on Sustainable Development (CSD) was established in December 1992 to ensure effective follow-up to UNCED. This commission was established to monitor and report on the implementation of the agreements at the local, national, regional, and international levels. It was agreed that a five-year review of the progress of the Earth Summit would be undertaken by the United Nations General Assembly in special session in 1997.

The full implementation of Agenda 21, the program for further implementation of Agenda 21 and the commitments to the Rio Principles were strongly reaffirmed at the World Summit on Sustainable Development - World Summit on Sustainable Development (WSSD) - held in Johannesburg, South Africa, from August 26 to September 4, 2002.

Agenda 2030

Current global climate policy, whose main goal is to reduce CO_2 emissions, is based on Agenda 2030. This agenda includes an intensification of policies already initiated in 1992. United Nations Agenda 2030 was adopted in September 2015 by all 193 participating countries and is described as a universal framework for all countries to eliminate poverty and achieve "sustainable" development by 2030.[2] However, Agenda 2030 does not only include climate-related policies. The agenda includes 17 so-called Sustainable Development Goals (SDGs), also known as Global Goals, of which climate is just one. It will be clear that Agenda 2030 requires not only big changes but also big investments. For the purposes of this book, only wind energy investments that fall under the "climate" SDG will be discussed. And indeed, these are substantial and give only a small indication of the total investments needed to implement the entire climate agenda.

The United Nations Sustainable Development Goals

The 17 SDGs, launched by the United Nations in 2015, are a universal call to action to end poverty, protect the planet and ensure that all people on Earth can live in peace and prosperity by 2030. At first glance, this seems like an extremely noble goal. However, further study quickly reveals that there are quite a few snags in this non-voluntary policy and there may even be a hidden agenda. Indeed, in addition to reducing CO_2 emissions, the SDGs also cover issues such as gender neutrality (the woke culture), control over food and healthcare and the further digitization of the world. These goals cannot all be covered in this book, but in practice they amount to far-reaching measures that will be taken to force people to do something that in most cases they have not chosen for themselves and that, for all sorts of reasons, are also not at all in the interest of people, animals, and the planet. I will give some examples of this later in this chapter.

By all accounts, the SDGs seem to lead primarily to far-reaching government control of humanity. Indeed, except for a small elite exempted, the SDGs allow the introduction of more and more freedom-restricting measures. The first signs include the "social credit system" (first introduced in China); the 15-minute cities (where freedom of movement is drastically curtailed); the ever-increasing taxation of (car) mobility, housing, savings, energy and food; the curtailment and criminalization of criticism of the government; the abolition of cash money (with the first limitation on the amount of transactions), a basic income (on strict conditions), the introduction of a digital currency (CBDC), a use-by date for digital money (to make saving impossible), control of digital transactions starting at 100 Euros (later 0.01 Euros), etc.

We have already seen (road) transportation, automobility, air travel, energy consumption of homes and industrial production become significantly more expensive in a very short period. How this will achieve the goal of ending poverty remains to be seen. The question of whether this is indeed an intended goal is therefore highly relevant and justified.

Critics argue that the desired control society will only serve the interests of government and big business. The self-employed - the small and medium-sized businesses, the independent middle class, farmers, and fishermen - must go away as soon as possible, and that is what we see happening around us right now. The ordinary citizen is being reduced, at best as a cash cow of the Agenda, easily controlled, with no freedom and no say. And all this to save the planet.

European Green Deal

From Agenda 2030, the so-called "European Green Deal" has emerged. This is led by Dutch Eurocommissioner Wopke Hoekstra, as substitute for Fran Timmermans. The Green Deal[3] is the core priority of the von der Leyen Commission and aims to make Europe the first climate-neutral continent. This should be done in a fair and social way. The Green Deal elaborates European policy on CO_2 emissions.

Climate neutral in itself is a rather unusual, new term. It means that a government, organization or process no longer emits CO_2 or, if that is not possible, its CO_2 emissions are offset. Offsetting is what is (should be) chosen most often in practice. Companies can then simply continue with their current production processes and the associated CO_2 emissions, if, in addition, they invest in projects of compensation organizations. The activity involved in CO_2 offsetting is booming business for consulting firms. More on this in Chapter 5.

The Climate Law adopted by the European Council on June 28, 2021, is at the heart of the European Green Deal. By laying down the climate goals in laws and regulations, the Climate Law gives direction to European climate policy for the next 30 years. As a result, the Climate Act is also known as the "Law of Laws". To reduce greenhouse gas emissions to zero by 2050, according to the Green Deal, the European Union will have to emit 55% less CO_2 compared to 1990 as early as 2030. The European Commission should aim for negative emissions by 2050.

The European Commission's "Fit for 55" climate package is supposed to provide that 55% CO_2 reduction. This climate package was adopted in July 2021 as part of the Green Deal and Agenda 2030. [4]

As can be seen, European policy is mainly characterized by a rather forced top-down approach. The EU implements policy mainly by adopting directives. These directives are implemented in national legislation and then embedded in national, regional and local decision-making. Through this route, therefore, municipalities, provinces and water boards all must deal with European environmental policy in practice.[5]

Dutch climate policy

Together with some other European member states, the Netherlands, always the best boy in the class, is leading the way with goals that will have a very profound effect on society. For example, the Netherlands has set high climate ambitions - or rather, CO_2-ambitions. The central government first stated that CO_2 emissions must be reduced by 55% from 1990 levels by 2030, as a prelude to a climate-neutral Netherlands by 2050. In June 2022, the Netherlands presented its climate policy program that targets as much as a 60% reduction in CO_2 emissions by 2030 (using 1990 as a reference). The government apparently considers an acceleration of emission reduction necessary for our small country. To achieve the tightened target of 55% reduction in 2030 with sufficient certainty, the government therefore wants to aim for even 60% emission reductions in the elaboration of climate policy, so that even in the event of setbacks, the 55% will be achieved.

This tightening of Dutch policy must deal, among other things, with the famous Urgenda verdict. Urgenda, founded in 2007, is a foundation for sustainability and innovation. Together with companies, governments, civil society organizations and individuals, Urgenda aims to make the Netherlands sustainable faster. On December 20, 2019, the Supreme Court issued its final ruling in Urgenda's climate case against the Dutch State. This forced the government to reduce CO_2 emissions at an accelerated pace.[6] Remarkably, the Urgenda case was heavily sponsored by, among others, the National Postcode Lottery, which at that time had already transferred Urgenda over 8 million euros.

When it comes to the SDGs, the Netherlands is obviously leading the way with its goals as well. No fewer than 117 municipalities have declared themselves Global Goals municipalities. This means that they have drawn up a joint action plan to work on the SDGs, make the necessary resources available for this and then involve as many residents, businesses, and organizations as possible. Although the other municipalities do not express themselves in this way, they face the same mandatory Agenda through European regulations. After all, this automatically works through the central government and the Provincial States.

In fact, countries that support the SDGs and signed the treaty entered a contract in 2015. There seems to be no turning back. Recently, the consequences have begun to become more and more apparent. In the Netherlands, for example, we have suddenly faced a nitrogen crisis. Linked to that are the buyouts of farmers, extremely high energy prices, an asylum crisis and historically high inflation. All these crises seem superficially isolated. However, a closer look reveals that they fit seamlessly with the goals of Agenda 2030 and the SDGs. As always, in times of crisis it becomes possible to accelerate all kinds of unpopular measures. We saw this very well, for example, during the covid crisis.

The clearly created nitrogen crisis [after all, in our neighboring countries, just across the border, totally different standards apply] is another excellent example. In May 2019, the Council of State ruled that the government, which is responsible for the nitrogen emission reduction policy, was functioning inadequately. After the highest administrative court drew a line under the nitrogen policy, building, living, and doing business in the Netherlands suddenly became a whole lot more difficult. That was the birth of the nitrogen crisis.[7] The nitrogen measures on the table in the summer of 2023 mean that farmers will have to be bought out. This would have been unthinkable had there not been a crisis. However, the buyout measures align with one of the SDGs, which is to reduce global meat consumption and reduce livestock. Instead of meat, using the SDG in question at the same time, there is a sudden push to eat insects as a substitute for human need for protein. The suggestion that there may be a coordinated action here is not far-fetched.

By raising energy prices, a government can effectively force people to use less energy. Using subsidies - as an alternative to simply mandating something by law - people can be encouraged to switch to, say, a heat pump. In this way, however, the electrification of the energy supply is disproportionately increased. After all, experts indicate that our electricity grid is not suitable for so many heat pumps. To this will soon be added the necessary electric charging stations for electric cars. The consequences this will have on the power grid are discussed in detail in Chapter 5.

The exorbitant increase in energy prices in late 2022 was associated with the war in Ukraine. The criticism of this showed that the prices were rather artificially raised by the big energy concerns that saw in the crisis - never waste a good crisis - an excellent opportunity to increase their profits. For example, oil and gas group Shell posted record profits of 38.4 billion euros for 2022. The group's highest profit in 115 years. The American oil group ExxonMobil surpassed this with a profit of 51 billion euros for 2022. In other countries, energy prices rose much less or not at all. Rather, it seemed that the energy groups, together with the government that increased the energy tax from 9% to as much as 21% in the same period, wanted to invest the extra money from Dutch citizens in wind and solar farms.

In any case, the knife to serve the SDGs cut both ways. First, high energy prices dampened energy consumption - and thus CO_2 emissions - and second, an acceleration in the transition to solar and wind power could come about due to the high prices of energy leading to higher revenues for governments and energy corporations.

Regional Energy Strategy

Global climate goals have been translated in the Netherlands into the 2018 Climate Agreement, which is a derivative of Agenda 2030. The Netherlands has placed direction for the implementation of the climate agenda with the National Regional Energy Strategy Program (RES).[8] Each region within the RES is governed by members of

Provincial Councils, water boards, municipal councils, and delegates from energy companies. Councilors of municipalities sometimes also have prominent positions within governing bodies of the RES. [9]

One requirement of the Climate Agreement is that 50% of the energy generated be locally owned. That means lobbying for residents of municipalities to co-invest in an energy cooperative that will install wind turbines, for example. The Climate Accord also stipulates that 30 regions must generate a total of 35 TWh of renewable electricity by 2030 - 1 TWh, or terrawatt hours, equals 1 billion kWh. That's about a third of our current electricity consumption each year.

To put this amount of electricity in perspective a few numbers: an average household consumes about 2.500 kWh annually, a city like Amsterdam consumes about 3.8 TWh of electricity per year, of which 1 TWh is consumed by households. The rest goes mainly to offices and industry, including large data centers. An average factory in the Netherlands consumes 150.000 kWh annually.

The Netherlands has 4 coal-fired power plants, generating an average of 1.000 MW of electricity. This corresponds to an annual average of 8.76 TWh of electricity per coal-fired plant, assuming full operation. A 3 MW wind turbine generates an average of 7 GWh of electricity annually. To completely replace one coal-fired power plant with wind turbines, a total of 1.251 3 MW wind turbines need to be operational.

Fig. 3.1: Horizon pollution from tall wind turbines near the town of Urk.

How many wind turbines do we actually need?

What the government has systematically failed to do is explain exactly how many wind turbines are needed for the energy transition. Nowhere at all is it explained that this will be a huge number of wind turbines and that this will have an enormous impact on the immediate living environment of practically every Dutch person. Because building wind turbines on land costs about two to three times less than building at sea, by far the most wind turbines will be placed on land. I discuss this in more detail later in this book.

A March 2022 report by research organization TNO shows how the Netherlands will be filled with wind turbines.[10] Figure 3.2 shows the map of the Netherlands, on which the wind turbines that have already been realized are drawn; next to them are the wind turbines that are planned on land for the realization of the RES until 2030 (the green dots). What is striking is the accuracy with which the wind turbines yet to be realized are already plotted. This while provinces and municipalities in most cases have yet to officially begin the procedures for determining search areas for the placement of wind turbines.

With the above information, one can get an impression of the enormous task facing the RES. With the so-called RES 1.0, a foundation has been laid for regional cooperation to contribute to the Climate Agreement. With this, the administrative partners in the RES indicate what they want to contribute to the energy transition and how they want to work together with residents and social organizations in a regional context to achieve these goals. To generate sufficient energy with wind turbines and solar parks by 2030, the necessary permits must be issued by early 2025 at the latest. At that time, therefore, it should also be clear where wind and solar farms can be realized. New agreements with municipalities will be laid down in the RES 2.0, on which decisions will be taken in the summer of 2023 in both the municipal councils, the Provincial States, and general boards of the water boards. Following a decision on RES 2.0, the next phase, RES 3.0, will start immediately.

In practice, therefore, the RES faces a choice between either wind or solar. The RES has chosen to realize 60% wind energy and 40% solar energy by 2030. One reason for this is the cost of connection to the electricity grid. Nationwide, a ratio of 80% solar and 20% wind is currently realized. This increases the pressure on the RES to accelerate the realization of more wind turbines. Since the realization of a wind farm takes seven to ten years, people are diligently looking for regions where large wind farms can be built.

Once these sites are identified by provinces and municipalities, what is known as an EIA (environmental impact assessment) procedure must be initiated. The first step in this process is the preparation of a "Notitie Reikwijdte en Detailniveau" (NRD). The NRD describes which themes and environmental effects should be investigated in the EIA procedure. In addition, the NRD provides information on how the environmental impacts will be studied and their depth. The second step is then the preparation of a *planEIA,* the environmental impact report. A *planEIR* examines environmental effects for the region in outline form.

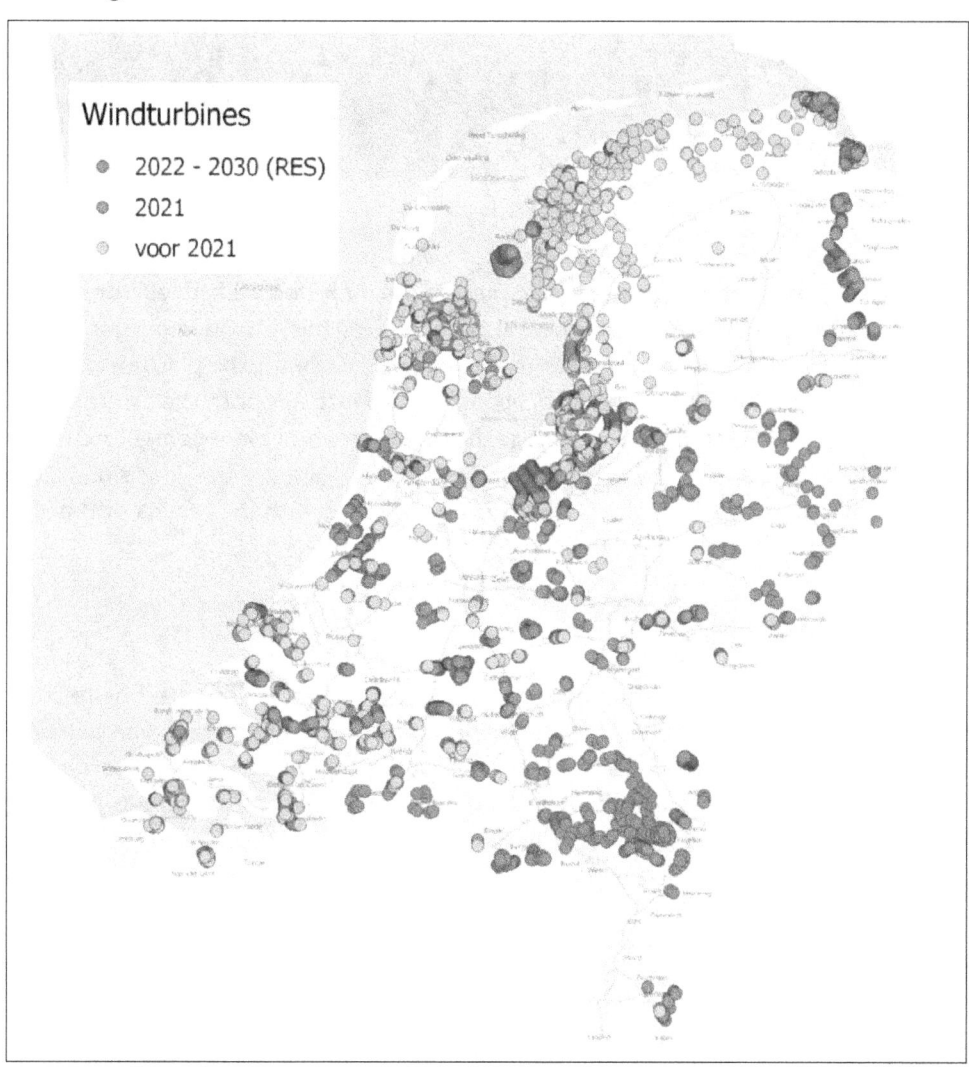

Fig. 3.2: Location of all wind turbines in the Netherlands (on land) by 2030, differentiated by time of placement. (Map data from the Basic Registration of Topography (BRT)).

Fig. 3.3: The new Dutch landscape.[11]

The study according to the *planEIA* must provide insight into what positive and/or negative environmental effects will take place if the intended objectives from the RES 1.0 are realized. From an environmental perspective, this provides insight into the areas that are suitable, can be made suitable or unsuitable for the placement of wind turbines. The result of the study will be incorporated into a report, the environmental impact report. This is an obligation under the Environmental Management Act.[12] This report is usually prepared by a consulting firm and is not a political decision. It is up to the administrators to weigh up what they want to do with the results of the study during the decision-making process.

Oudeschip, East Groningen

The impact and implementation of the policy in practice are described by residents of the village of Oudeschip in eastern Groningen in an article by Irene van der Linde. That article was published July 14, 2021, in magazine *'De Groene Amsterdammer'* and describes how the inhabitants of Oudeschip see the natural polder landscape slowly changing into an industrial landscape with wind turbines. The village of Oudeschip with about 250 inhabitants, is the northernmost village in the Netherlands. The village lies on the edge of the Oostpolder with the Eemshaven to the north of it with an area of 600 hectares. This polder used to be an idyllic Dutch landscape. Now, from 600 meters away from the village edge, it is filled with 21 wind turbines of 223 meters tip height. "Anyone can figure out that there is a big story behind this," writes a resident of the village to the newspaper's editor, who continues with: "It is not a question for our defense, but for clarification what forces are at play here."

Fig. 3.4: Wind turbines at Eemshaven - David cannot stand up to so many Goliaths ...

In 2021, it emerged that the province of Groningen and the municipality of Hogeland (which includes Oudeschip) had been developing plans to expand the Eemshaven industrial area into the Oostpolder since October 2019. This was done in the deepest secrecy, supposedly "to prevent land speculation". 'In confidence,' the province and municipality had market surveys conducted. When the outcome was overwhelmingly positive, it was decided to start implementing "a master plan". Sometime in April 2021, the residents' letter with the government message fell on everyone's doorstep. Residents were stunned. The new developments effectively heralded the end of Oudeschip. The villagers - regardless of whether they are for or against the new plans - all feel cheated and unheard. They have completely lost confidence in the province and municipality. It turned out that the land in the Oostpolder had been sold to Google. Government officials abused their powers, duped a local farmer and secretly awarded wind turbine rights worth millions to the main landowner.

By the time the villagers were informed about the placement of 21 wind turbines, everything was basically in the works. All that remained was the possibility of submitting an opinion and a notice of objection. Whether these were read at all remains the big question.

In the 1970s, the area near Oudeschip was still a rich bird migration area, but that is long gone. Now digging and construction is going on 24 hours a day. TenneT is laying new high-voltage power lines and building new pylons to transport the large amount of energy that comes ashore here from the wind farms above Schiermonnikoog to Groningen.

This example of how the agenda is rolled out across the community in practice is catchily typified by the following statements from one of Oudeschip's residents:

"Deputies and councilors come and go. All want to assert themselves here. It goes over us like a wave and every time we must get back on the ropes. They hire expensive consultancies from the West, with boys and girls sitting behind computers, devising plans about our polder. The violence of intelligence. They are smart and sophisticated. Talking current language, using words we don't know. Our adaptability is called upon all the time. We are constantly faced with changes. There is no peace in the environment. I am constantly on my guard: what will happen next? People say: you must move with the times, standing still is going backwards. I wonder to what extent that is true."

As the above example indicates, it is not hard to imagine that the RES's modus operandi plays into turning people against each other. After all, no one wants a wind farm in his or her immediate neighborhood. People in rural areas are getting at each other within the municipal boundaries. People who live along the canal want the wind turbines in the meadows and people who live in the meadows prefer the wind turbines along the canal. The winners in this battle are the operators of the wind turbines. The RES ultimately transfers responsibility for permitting to the municipalities. About the plans forged with double agendas the residents are then only informed afterwards. In fact, most people do not even know of the existence of the RES. By then, the decisions have already been made and the so-called consultation round for residents is just a formality. A curtain call. What remains for the residents then is to start costly legal proceedings, or to ensure that the wind turbines are built at another location within the municipal boundaries. Or relocate.

The consequences of Dutch climate policy

In addition to the most visible effects of climate policy for all to see, namely the explosion of wind turbines and solar farms, the measures resulting from the policy are rapidly succeeding.

In 2022, for example, the Dutch government devised a new rule requiring companies with more than 100 employees to first monitor and then report the CO_2 emissions of their staff. This new rule took effect on Jan. 1, 2023. Companies that overexceed the maximum emission standard are given four years to reduce their CO_2 emissions.

For organizations and their staff, lowering those emissions may mean tighter controls on staff travel and commuting. It may also mean steering a change in commuting toward lower-emission mobility, such as biking, public transportation, electric vehicles or simply reducing the distances traveled. In short, this will make it immediately clear what the consequences of the policy will be.

So it starts first with monitoring, which in itself still seems fairly innocuous. However, there are already systems on the market, such as Travel Balance, which also record privacy-sensitive information. This allows each employee to be monitored for his or her CO_2 emissions when commuting. This will eventually lead to an (in)direct compulsion to drive electric or use public transportation. For people who live in rural areas, have poor access to public transportation and do not want to get into an electric car or simply cannot afford one, this ultimately means that they will be "punished" for their CO_2 emissions. Their colleagues will be rewarded for their good behavior; the employee in question will miss out on his reward or be penalized financially, which will create a huge skew in working conditions.

The first obligations that will affect many people have also been announced. The first is the mandatory installation of a hybrid heat pump from 2026. The second is the from 2025 mandatory installation of solar panels on new buildings with a roof area of 250 square meters or more. The third is the ban on the sale of new gasoline and diesel cars from 2035.[13] This will force residents in the Netherlands to make huge investments. For a hybrid heat pump, investment costs can be as much as 10.000 euros or more, depending on the size and insulation value of the home. The average purchase price of an electric car in 2022 was more than 50% higher than that of a gasoline car.[14] This is aside from the fact that the benefit in the amount of road tax expires on January 1, 2025.

In addition, the heat pump itself turns out not to be that environmentally friendly at all. A February 2023 article, in which new calculations for the National Environmental Database were published, shows that the materials used in a heat pump are more harmful than previously thought.[15] The calculations show that the environmental impact of producing and reusing the materials in a heat pump, among other things, is 11 times higher than previously considered, according to NED's article.[16] To avoid ambiguity, delay or downtime in home construction, the NED Foundation has come up with a temporary solution. Until the effects of all heat pumps are mapped, a settlement factor is in effect, which broadly amounts to keeping the old environmental scores for now.

It won't just be about mandatory heat pumps and solar panels on roofs. In fact, the government has decided to take firmer control of climate policy. For all sectors, the government will set a residual emission target, which will make clear the maximum amount of emissions a certain sector may still emit in 2030. The ministers involved are the Minister of the Domestic Affairs and Kingdom Relations, the Minister of Nature and Nitrogen, the Minister of Housing and Spatial Planning, the Minister of Agriculture, Nature and Food Quality, the Minister of Economic Affairs and Climate Change, the Minister of Finance, the Minister of Infrastructure and Water Management, the State Secretary for Taxation and the State Secretary for Infrastructure and Water Management. They are responsible for achieving this goal in their own sectors and the coordinating minister for Climate and Energy monitors the progress and coherence of the implementation of overall climate policy. [17]

The Cabinet also paved the way for a so-called scientific Climate Council by Royal Decree on Oct. 29, 2022.[18] A Royal Decree is a decision the government can make outside the States General - the elected representatives of the people in the Senate and House of Representatives. This decree makes it relatively easy for the government to fill influential positions, including the appointment of mayors. This scientific advisory council, which is supposed to be independent, will consist of 8 to 10 members who will assess and advise on climate policy, solicited and unsolicited.

As in countless other cases, the government relies for its policies on the advisory councils it appoints, by Royal Decree, which include so-called experts. These are often people with high positions, people in influential positions and with a certain social prestige. Critics will say that these are mainly people who will support government policy, something we saw before with the covid crisis. So such advisory councils do not come about democratically, but in many cases they turn out to be decisive for the policies to be implemented.

1. sustainabledevelopment.un.org/outcomedocuments/agenda21
2. sdgs.un.org/2030agenda
3. europadecentraal.co.uk/european-green-deal-the-way-to-climate-neutrality/
4. ec.europa.eu/commission/presscorner/detail/en/IP_21_3541
5. europadecentraal.com/topic/climate-and-environment/environment-policy/
6. www.rijksoverheid.nl/documenten/publicaties/2022/06/02/ontwerp-beleidsprogramma-klimaat;%20www.urgenda.nl
7. Book 'Green is the new red' from Culture Under Fire - Civitas Christiana Foundation
8. www.regionale-energiestrategie.nl/default.aspx
9. www.rtvoost.nl/nieuws/1877687/straks-94-windmolens-en-honderden-voetbalvelden-aan-zonnepanelen-in-noordwesten-overijssel
10. TNO report TNO 2022 P10374; "The expected impact of wind turbines on house prices in the Netherlands. A spatial analysis for the period 2020-2030," March 3, 2022
11. pxhere.com/en/photo/638728
12. wetten.overheid.nl/BWBR0003245/2019-01-01
13. www.europarl.europa.eu/news/en/headlines/economy/20221019STO44572/eu-ban-on-sale-of-new-petrol-and-diesel-cars-from-2035-explained
14. www.autoweek.nl/autonieuws/artikel/elektrische-auto-gemiddeld-54-procent-duurder-dan-auto-op-benzine/
15. nos.nl/artikel/2464758-materials-in-heat-pumps-damaging-more-damaging-for-environment-than-thought
16. environmentaldatabase.co.uk/en/actual/news/environmental-tax- heat-pump-falls-higher-out/
17. www.rijksoverheid.nl/actueel/nieuws/2022/06/02/kabinet-presenteert-beleidsprogramma-klimaat
18. search.officialinformation.com/stb-2022-432.html

Fig. 3.5: In more and more places, the natural landscape must give way completely to industrial wind energy: people and animals have nothing left to do there.

Fig. 3.6: The modern wind turbine is a Mega Structure.

HVDC DolWin2 Beta platform for the transmission of wind power from the German part of the North Sea. (Wikipedia)

Chapter 4: Climate change?

Our Earth's climate is perhaps the most talked about topic in the West today. Not a day goes by without something new being reported about the climate. The thesis that humans are to blame for changing that climate and that, therefore, the current generation must come up with solutions to save future generations from catastrophe is examined in more detail in this chapter.

Code red for climate

The distress call for human intervention in the climate is not something of recent years. For decades reasons have been put forward as to why intervention would be necessary. In the 1970s, for example, there were warnings of a new ice age;[1] in the 1980s it was acid rain that would prove catastrophic and in the 1990s the warnings of global warming began. Again and again, new generations are confronted with climate doom stories. The media play a key role in this climate alarmism. Articles place the responsibility for the climate entirely on man, so this process has been going on for at least 50 years.

Similarly, several articles were published in the Netherlands in the 1970s in which so-called "experts" indicated that we could expect a new ice age. At the time, KNMI claimed that the world had been getting colder for about ten years: "The drop in temperature is small, no more than half a degree Celsius so far, but the consequences are enormous," it said. The media take it over without criticism. On January 28, 1974, for example, De Leeuwarder Courant carried the following:

> "Leading meteorologists from all parts of the world are convinced that the earth is slowly moving toward a new ice age," after which the article ends with: "For climatologists, these are indications of drastic changes in the Earth's climate, which - if it continues - could become of paramount importance to humanity, they believe."

Just as quickly as these reports appeared, they disappeared again to make way for the acid rain of the 1980s. Heightened by the media, the acid rain hype justified governments introducing all kinds of legislation for industry and farmers to reduce emissions of nitrogen and sulfur compounds in particular. After all, these would be the cause of dying forests.

Hegelian thought
It is important to note here that many policies in our society come about in the following way: a crisis is created by the government, after which the media exaggerate the fear of that crisis. Then that same government comes up with a solution to the crisis. Hegel calls this *problem - reaction - solution*. What we always see is that certain

stakeholders benefit from the desired solution. After all, the solutions always cost a lot of money - the bill, by definition, is placed on the citizen - and all that money goes somewhere. The result is that the difference between rich and poor in our world is widening and at the same time people's freedom is diminishing, because of all kinds of new legislation that the government (which caused the problem) believes is necessary to fight the "crisis."

Stories about warming didn't start well until after the 1992 United Nations Conference on Environment and Development in Rio de Janeiro, where a climate treaty was concluded. In the 21st century, climate propaganda then gained momentum through the mainstream media. It starts with U.S. Vice President Al Gore, who in 2006 published his book titled "An Inconvenient Truth: The Planetary Emergency of Global Warming and What We Can Do About It," with which he toured the world. The docufilm of the same name reached a large audience. Gore made all kinds of predictions for the planet and humanity as a result of man-made climate change.

Al Gore

Albert Arnold (Al) Gore Jr. is a former American politician of the Democratic Party. He was the vice president from 1993-2001 under President Bill Clinton and he lost the 2000 presidential election against G.W. Bush.[2] His book received tremendous media attention. Along with the United Nations Intergovernmental Panel on Climate Change (IPCC), he was awarded the Nobel Peace Prize in 2007 *"for increasing and disseminating knowledge about human-caused climate change and for promoting measures to counter it."*

Now almost 20 years on, it appears that many of Al Gore's predictions have not come true. For example, according to Al Gore, Kilimanjaro in Africa should have already been free of snow, which did not happen. Also, according to Al Gore, more extreme weather events such as storms and hurricanes should have occurred. That hasn't happened. We know this because accurate records of storms have been kept in the United States since 1959. Figure 4.1 shows that the number of storms worldwide did not increase from 1981 to 2021.[3] There is no upward trend in either number or intensity there: the number and intensity of storms have been stable for 40 years.

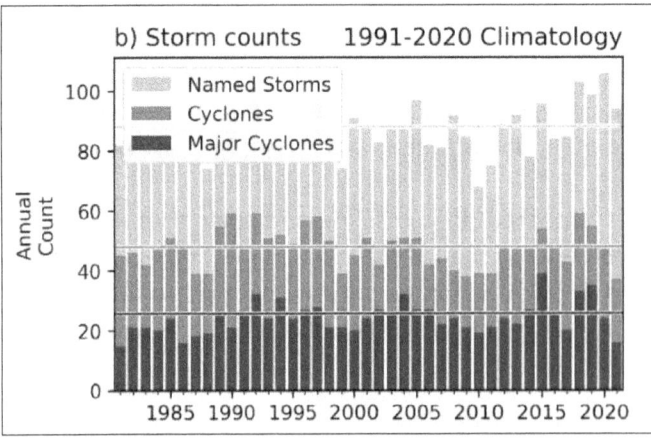

Fig. 4.1: The global number of storms and severe storms from 1991 to 2020.

In addition, early in this century, Gore predicted that "The North Pole will be absolutely ice-free by 2015." This prediction, too, is now in the graveyard. Especially after very early in the fall of 2021-2022, a large convoy of cargo ships froze much earlier than normal in the northern waters over Russia. In fact, on May 13, 2022, the area of Arctic ice was as large as it was on May 13, 1989.[4]

With his prediction of the polar bear population extinction, the exact opposite happened: there are more polar bears than ever. The polar bear population has grown dramatically in recent decades: from 5,000 in the 1960s to about 30,000 today.[5] Gore also warned of a disruption of the warm Gulf Stream due to freshwater inflows from melting Greenland ice and melting North American glaciers. The alarming signs at the glaciers of Glacier National Park in the United States, which said that because of man-made global warming, visitors were the last ones to see all that beauty, have since been taken down. The climate models' predictions that they would have melted by now were not entirely correct.

Even Dutch weatherman Reinier van den Berg, made the statement in 2012 that the Arctic would be ice-free by 2015 in summer. 2012 was the year that the Arctic ice surface had reached a temporary low. Typical of current climate alarmism is that when an "extreme" weather event takes place or when a "record" is broken, the alarm is immediately raised. It is important to remember here that weather data have only been kept for a geologically relatively short period of time - namely since 1901 - with which to validate models. For this reason, it is not surprising that the occasional daily or annual record is broken. After all, climate is the weather over long periods of time; weather is the state of the atmosphere now. Climate and weather are therefore completely different and cannot (and should not) be compared.

Since 2018, Greta Thunberg has become the face of a global movement to fight climate change. Already at the age of seventeen, she motivated millions of people around the world to participate in protests; to call on governments to act on climate change and to hold corporations accountable for it. According to Greta Thunberg,

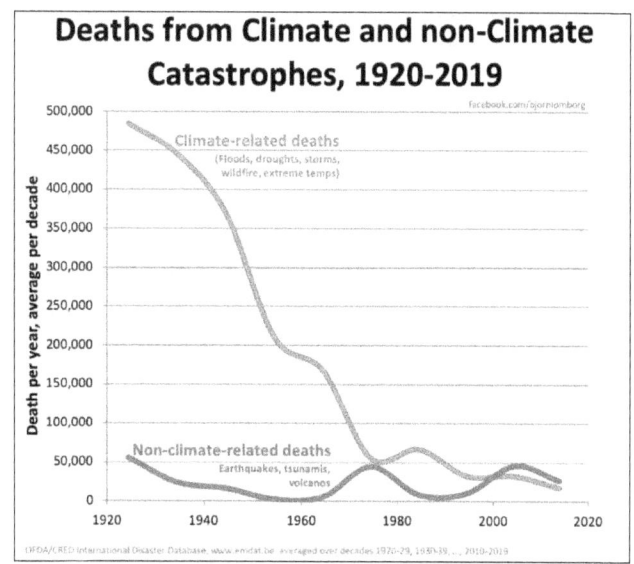

Fig. 4.2: The number of climate-related and non-climate-related deaths over the period 1920-2019.[7]

people are dying because of climate change, *"People are dying"* became one of her most famous statements, uttered on September 23, 2019 at the United Nations Climate Action Summit in New York, where she received the highest podium.[6] That things do look different in reality, as figures show, does not negate the fact that a huge fear has been created with this kind of statement, after which a large group of people have rallied behind this, to say the least, questionable narrative. Of course, courtesy of the mainstream media.

Figure 4.2 shows the evolution of climate and non-climate related deaths over the last hundred years. Since 1920 the number of deaths from climate-related natural disasters has declined dramatically and continues to decline. This can be attributed to the increased prosperity in the world. In fact, people are increasingly able to protect themselves against such natural disasters. Among other things, all kinds of warning systems have been developed, dikes and flood defenses have been built, water level regulation systems exist, and houses have been made resistant to earthquakes. These developments made possible by increased prosperity have thus ensured that humans are increasingly protected against natural disasters, especially those related to climate. The above paints a completely different picture than what is shouted by governments, media and climate activists. Humanity is not threatened with extinction because the Earth's temperature has increased by 1.1°C since 1850. On the contrary, the figures show that we are increasingly resilient to natural disasters and have adapted excellently to the natural fluctuations of the climate.

CO_2 and the climate

The United Nations cites as the main argument for phasing out fossil fuels such as oil, natural gas, coal, and lignite that their combustion contributes significantly to CO_2 levels in the Earth's atmosphere. Environmentalists (including the many scientists) claim that CO_2 causes global warming, and this is their main dogma. The average temperature of the air and oceans would be increasing due to increasing concentrations of greenhouse gases (not only CO_2 but also methane, for example) resulting from human activities, such as the burning of fossil fuels, as well as agriculture and deforestation. The question, however, is whether this is indeed the case.

Ice cores have been examined at the Russian research base Vostok in Antarctica. The ice contains geological information of thousands of years. This research has shown that CO_2 is not the cause of temperature rise, but rather an increase in CO_2 levels in the Earth's atmosphere is the result of temperature rise. Researchers were able to show through measurements on the ice that CO_2 levels on Earth lag temperature by about 800 years each time. If the Earth's temperature rises for a long time, the CO_2 content will also rise about 800 years later.[8] This 800-year lag is because the temperature of Earth's oceans determines the increase or decrease of CO_2 in the atmosphere. Given the enormous volumes of water in the oceans, it takes a very long time for an increase in atmospheric temperature to pass through to the oceans. When the temperature of the oceans increases, they release more CO_2 to the atmosphere and vice versa, when the temperature drops, the oceans absorb more CO_2.[9]

That global warming would be caused by CO_2 is also refuted by looking at our written history. Indeed, during the medieval warming period, the so-called "Medieval

Warm Period," temperatures in Europe were higher than they are today. Grapes were grown in northern England and crops and meadows flourished in now icy Greenland - after all, according to the Vikings, it was a "green land".

From the 16th century to the mid-19th century, there was a "little ice age" on Earth. Chronicles tell how people skated on the frozen Thames. The warming trend that started from the year 1850 was then interrupted again by a significant cooling between 1940 and 1970. Hence the alarmism in the 1970s about a new ice age. Precisely in the period '40-'70 there were huge industrial developments that involved an explosive increase in the use of fossil fuels. So that directly contradicts the direct relationship between warming and CO_2.

Thus, contrary to continuous claims, CO_2 is not the cause of the current period of global warming. The main greenhouse gas (if the greenhouse effect were to exist at all) is water vapor. In some places and at some times its concentration is up to a hundred times higher than that of CO_2.

In addition, research has shown that solar activity and the oceans are the main regulators of global climate. But there are also other factors such as volcanic eruptions and incoming cosmic rays. Volcanic eruptions throw cubic kilometers of dust (aerosols) into the atmosphere. Those dust particles form the nuclei on which water molecules can deposit; that leads to cloud formation and clouds cause cooling etc. Cosmic rays, in turn, also have an ionizing effect in the atmosphere: molecules can be split, and this has major implications for cloud formation, among other things. In short, there are quite a few factors outside of humans that have a much greater impact on climate.

Incidentally, it is also hard to imagine that an increase in a natural gas that is only 0.042% (420 ppm) in our atmosphere could have catastrophic consequences for the Earth. Indeed, in a sense, CO_2, like oxygen, is a life gas. Humans and animals feed fundamentally on plants. Plants absorb CO_2 from the atmosphere through photosynthesis. In the process, starch, sugars, and fiber are produced. The "byproduct" of photosynthesis is the oxygen we breathe. In the highly unlikely event - but at the same time the desired scenario of the environmental movement - that we would be able to remove all CO_2 from the atmosphere, life on Earth would simply cease to exist. And in fact, much earlier, namely at levels below 100 ppm, or 0.01% of atmospheric gases.

In summary, Earth's climate is not simply the result of "the greenhouse effect" or "the concentration of CO_2". It is the product of everything in the universe (sunlight and cosmic rays) and its interaction with our planet. Maintaining a clean environment is necessary for the survival of humanity, but it is independent of climate change.

Despite all the above, to emphasize the artificial necessity for implementing climate policies, the Intergovernmental Panel on Climate Change (IPCC) was established in 1988 by the World Meteorological Organization and the United Nations Environment Program.

The IPCC

The IPCC plays a key role in shaping global climate policy. The IPCC was established to provide policymakers with regular scientific assessments of the current state of knowledge on climate change. The IPCC completed its sixth assessment cycle in March 2023, publishing the assessment reports of its three working groups - three special reports - as early as 2021 and 2022. The fourth report, The Synthesis Report, a summary for policymakers, was published in March 2023.

The main steering body of the IPCC is the Executive Board (IPCC Bureau), which consists of 34 people and is elected by political representatives of the 195 member states. So, the top management level is determined politically, not scientifically. The fact that the environmental ministries of many countries are green and that most countries that make up the IPCC receive money from the UN Green Climate Fund directly reflects on the composition and interests of the governing body. The IPCC board then chooses the lead authors of the report. This gives the board great influence over the direction and content of the reports. Even if there are movements among the author requests with a wide range of opinions, the board can promote certain views and suppress others. They say there is diversity in terms of gender and regional origin, but not in terms of the diverse views and opinions within the climate debate. In other words, critics of the alarmist line would be excluded. And should they unexpectedly become authors, they would be quite isolated.

On the other hand, IPCC authors include numerous representatives of climate activists such as Greenpeace. Industry reporters are rare anyway. There are also some climate activists among the climate data report authors, such as from the Berlin-based think tank Climate Analytics, which in turn is supported by Greenpeace and the European Climate Foundation.

Patrick Moore, a founding member of Greenpeace, calls the IPCC "not a scientific organization," but a "political organization." "The IPCC hires scientists to provide them with 'information' that supports the 'climate emergency' narrative. Their campaigns against fossil fuels, nuclear power, CO_2, plastics, etc. are misguided and designed to make people think the world will perish unless we cripple our civilization and destroy our economy. They are now negatively impacting the future of both the environment and human civilization," Moore said.

So what about peer review of external experts? Those involved report that anyone can become an expert reviewer who has published in a relevant area of climato-logy. However, expert reviewers' comments are usually not addressed. In this way, no effective dialogue occurs.[10] Roger Pielke Jr. of the Cires Environmental Institute in Boulder, Colorado, complained that comments from expert reviewers were ignored without further explanation.[11]

About the impact of the IPCC reports on global climate policy, we can observe that they are extremely effective. Every time an IPCC report is published, the media are filled with climate alarmist reports that suggest to readers and viewers that the world will perish if we do not do something about the climate immediately. At the same time, the reports are welcomed by policymakers to further tighten policy, as evidenced by UN Secretary General Guterres' response to the March 2023 Synthesis Report.[12] "The climate time bomb is ticking," Guterres responded to the new report. He called on prosperous countries after the publication to achieve zero CO_2 emissions as early as 2040, 10 years ahead of schedule. Emerging economies should then achieve that goal around 2050. Coal use should also be curbed by then. Guterres: "Humanity is moving on thin ice. And that ice is melting fast."

However, we must return to the solutions presented to us to save humanity: back, therefore, to the role of wind energy in energy transition.

The logic

Looking at the numbers - and no complicated calculations are required - it immediately becomes clear that wind energy cannot possibly contribute to the United Nations' goals for reducing CO_2 emissions.

As an example, let's take the energy economy of the United States, using the year 2021 as a starting point. What exactly would it take to eliminate the use of fossil fuels in the US? Can wind energy ensure that CO_2 emissions are reduced to 0 - the famous Net Zero? The goal was to bring CO_2 emissions completely to zero by 2050. With that, we can calculate in three steps how many wind turbines are needed to achieve that. As mentioned, this calculation is limited to the United States, but similar calculations can be made for other countries. They will then differ in detail but not in principle.[13]

The first step is to determine the number of wind turbines needed to replace all electricity generated by fossil fuels in 2021. Wind generated 380 billion kWh in the U.S. in 2021, which was 9.2% of all electricity generated in the U.S. in 2021. The rated capacity of a wind turbine in the United States averages 2.5 megawatts. That number is based on a capacity factor of 32% for these turbines, which is the efficiency of the turbines relative to their maximum output. This allows us to calculate that by 2021, a total of 54.224 wind turbines should have been operational in the United States. So this is an estimate based on the rated capacity of a wind turbine. The actual number of wind turbines in 2021 may be slightly different from this. Since a starting point with fixed values is necessary to make the results of the calculations comparable, the theoretical approach was chosen here.

Now to determine the number of wind turbines needed to replace the total energy generated by coal and gas by 2050, these energy sources are added together. Coal accounted for 22% of energy production in the U.S. and gas provided 38% of total energy production. This means that the contribution to total energy production from coal and gas was 909 billion kWh and 1570 billion kWh, respectively. Taken together, this adds up to 2479 billion kWh. If we then divide this energy - in kWh - by the rated capacity that a wind turbine delivers annually - 7.008 GWh - we see that it would have taken 353.634 wind turbines to completely replace the energy generated by fossil fuels with wind turbines by 2021. [14][15]

So the situation in 2021 is known. However, the 2030 goals require all industrial production and transportation to be emission-free. That means, among other things, that all homes must be heated electrically, and cars and trucks must drive electrically. This requires - apart from the huge amount of additional charging stations - a huge amount of additional electricity. The second step will, therefore, determine how many new wind turbines will be needed if light vehicles are all fully electrically powered and if all homes are heated fully electrically instead of with natural gas. The "National Renewable Energy Lab" in the United States has calculated that the total amount of electricity needed will double when all light vehicles and home heating depend on electricity. Assuming this energy must be generated by wind turbines, this means an additional 4.130 TWh must be generated, the total amount of electricity generated in 2021. Using the same assumptions of 2.5 MW wind turbines and a capacity factor of 32%, it can be calculated that the number of wind turbines required to double the amount of electricity to be generated in 2050 thus comes to 589.391.[16]

But even that does not complete the whole picture of the number of wind turbines needed. Indeed, it also remains to be determined how many wind turbines are needed to generate enough hydrogen to produce steel and cement, assuming the goal of Net Zero CO_2 emissions. Little reliable data is available on the amount of hydrogen needed for cement production. However, sufficient data is available for the production of steel using hydrogen as the energy medium. The estimate given here for the number of wind turbines is based on the amount of hydrogen needed to produce 62 million tons of steel. This estimate excludes the amount of steel produced from metal waste and then - as a first order approximation - the number of wind turbines was doubled to compensate for cement production. In any case, the United States produced a total of 85.8 million tons of steel in 2021.[17]

Hydrogen is produced by electrolysis, a process that requires electricity. This is an estimate of the number of wind turbines required to generate this amount of electricity, which is 346 billion kWh. With an output of 7.008 GWh per year per wind turbine, the number of wind turbines needed comes to 49.365.

If we then add it all up, the number of additional wind turbines needed to achieve the goal of zero CO_2 emissions by 2050 is 353.634 + 589.391+ 49.365 = 992.390, rounded up to 1 million wind turbines.

The average number of wind turbines installed in a year in the United States was 3.000 after 2004.[18] That would mean that at this rate of construction, it would take 331 years to build the amount of wind turbines to meet the zero CO_2 goal. There was 1 year in which a maximum of 5.680 wind turbines were built. If we took that as a starting point, it would still take 175 years to build the required number of wind turbines. And that while they should be there by 2050, and there is only 29 years to do that, counting from 2021.

There are currently developments underway for the construction and installation of 5 MW wind turbines (in the calculation we assumed an average of 2.5 MW). However, the number of such wind turbines is currently zero. Assuming the possibility of installing 5 MW wind turbines in the US, 17.110 5 MW wind turbines would have to be built each year, over a period of 29 years until 2050. This rate of construction is still 3 times the maximum number of 2.5 MW turbines ever built in a single year.

But we are not there yet. In fact, more and more nuclear power plants are closing in the United States. The above calculations do not include the additional wind turbines needed to replace nuclear power with wind power.

And even then, we are not there yet. In fact, wind turbines have a lifespan of 20 years. That means that all existing wind turbines installed before 2022 must be replaced at some point before 2050. Replacement also applies to all wind turbines built between the present and 2030. These wind turbines also reach their useful life and are not included in the above calculations.[19]

In short, the calculations show that it is completely physically impossible to achieve the climate goals. Again, that is not being told to the citizen, neither by politicians, nor by science, nor by the media. However, the citizen must pay for the cost of the energy transition. A transition that, no matter what we do, is physically infeasible. So we must ask ourselves whether, with the Green Deals of this world, we are dealing with incompetence or a deliberate concealment of demonstrable facts. In the latter case, we need to ask ourselves what goals do lie behind initiatives such as the Green Deal.

1. Time Magazine article "Another Ice Age?", June 24, 1974; content.time.com/time/subscriber/article/0,33009,944914-1,00.html
2. en.wikipedia.org/wiki/List_of_vice_presidents_of_the_United_States
3. www.ncei.noaa.gov/access/monitoring/monthly-report/tropical-cyclones/202113#global-storms
4. National Snow & Ice Data Centre; nsidc.org/
5. www.arcticwwf.org/wildlife/polar-bear/polar-bear-population/
6. www.youtube.com/watch?v=N94eP2jKQWw
7. Lomborg, Bjørn, (2020), Welfare in the 21st century: Increasing development, reducing inequality, the impact of climate change, and the cost of climate policies, Technological Forecasting and Social Change, 156, issue C, number S0040162520304157
8. http://www.co2science.org/articles/V6/N26/EDIT.php; Professor Ian Clark
9. The Global Warming Swindle, producer Martin Durkin; www.youtube.com/watch?v=BY-gRF-SaP7o; Professor Carl Wunsch
10. www.climategate.nl/2022/05/wie-trekken-aan-de-touwtjes-achter-de-schermen-van-het-vn-klimaatpanel-ipcc/
11. rogerpielkejr.substack.com/p/misinformation-in-the-ipcc
12. nos.nl/collection/13871/article/2468251-again-ipcc-report-but-where-are-climate-scientists-actually-looking-at
13. "The Impossibility of Windmills": www.youtube.com/watch?v=-4qXeOe_35c&feature=youtu.be
14. www.statista.com/statistics/528603/distribution-electricity-net-generation-in-the-us-by-fuel-type/
15. www.statista.com/statistics/188521/total-us-electricity-net-generation/
16. www.nrel.gov/
17. www.statista.com/statistics/184535/crude-steel-production-in-the-us-since-2000/

18. www.usgs.gov/faqs/how-many-wind-turbines-are-installed-us-each-year
19. ddears.com/2022/05/18/net-zero-carbon-reality-check-1/

Chapter 5: The economic aspects of wind turbines

In our modern society, energy prices drive virtually all other prices. This is because everything we do requires energy. Not surprisingly, sharply rising energy prices are putting more and more households in financial trouble. For a long time, we have again known the phenomenon of "energy poverty," where people are left out in the cold because they can no longer pay their energy bills.

Meanwhile, the United Nations' climate agenda hidden in the SDGs involves countless of billions justified by telling humanity that the world will perish if immediate action is not taken. This has boosted economic activity around wind turbines. So there is literally a proliferation of wind trade. In 2021, for example, 41 billion euros was invested in the installation of new wind farms in Europe alone. According to Giles Dickson, CEO of WindEurope, each new offshore wind turbine generates €15 million in economic activity. WindEurope expects the 77.000 offshore wind jobs in Europe in 2020 to rise to 200.000 by 2030.[1]

Correctly determining the costs of all energy measures resulting from climate policy is extremely complex. The main problem here is that because of the numerous forms of subsidies, quite a few costs are hidden. It is not only the direct government support for investments in solar and wind energy and the use of biomass, but also favorable arrangements for the price of the energy purchased. For example, for the balancing scheme, guaranteed prices and not passing on the additional costs to be incurred by the grid.

With the information provided in this chapter on costs, financing, paper trading and the impact on the power grid, it is made clear that with the phasing out of fossil fuels and subsidizing investments in wind farms and solar meadows, today's society is in danger of getting into big trouble.

On top of the financial situations outlined in this chapter, politics can take a very dramatic turn in the energy market at any time. This happened as recently as 2022, for example, when the further closing of gas taps and the sanctions imposed on Russia by the European Union made European energy markets uncertain, causing energy prices to skyrocket. The conditions discussed in this chapter do not take such political events into account.

The cost of construction, installation, and operation of wind turbines

Chapter 2 made clear what is involved in the construction and installation of wind turbines. Not surprisingly, the costs involved are high. A modern land-based wind turbine has an average capacity of 3 MW. The investment cost for building and installing a 3 MW wind turbine on land is about 3.8 million euros.[2] When installed offshore, the costs are significantly higher than on land due to the complexity of construction and installation. Based on figures from the International Renewable Energy Agency (IRENA), the investment cost for a 9 MW offshore wind turbine is €29.6 million.[3] Per MW of power to be generated, it can thus be calculated that the cost of an offshore wind turbine is about three times higher than the cost of an onshore wind turbine.

The production of the turbines and foundations, including transportation and installation, account for approximately 70% of the total investment costs. Other costs include construction of civil engineering infrastructure, electrical infrastructure and grid connection, permits, development costs consisting of surveys and consulting, construction interest, insurance and disposal costs.

Exploitation

In addition to investment costs, there are operational costs. These amount to about 110.000 euros per year for a 3 MW wind turbine on land. The operational costs of a 9 MW wind turbine at sea run as high as 760.000 euros per year. [2]

What exactly do these operational costs consist of? First and foremost, operational costs include maintenance. The replacement of parts when they break down, for example, but also the maintenance contract with the turbine supplier or other parties. Second, there are operating costs, such as administration and accounting. After construction of the wind turbine, additional studies often need to be done, such as noise pollution in the vicinity of the turbine.

Operating costs also include what is known as the right of superficies. This is the rent paid by the owner of the wind turbine to the owner of the land on which the turbine stands. Although the amounts paid for the building rights are not public, there are indications that this amount is about 25 thousand euros per year for wind turbines on agricultural land and up to 40 thousand euros per year for wind turbines on government land.

Other operating costs also include insurance, self-use of electricity, property taxes, management costs and land and road maintenance. In some cases, costs for monitoring bird and bat casualties may also be added. In some areas, the government also asks for a contribution to the area development around the wind farm. In Flevoland in The Netherlands, for example, this amounts to as much as 10-30% of the annual yield of the wind farm.[4]

A municipality also incurs its own costs to respond to the placement of wind turbines. Think of policy preparation, the spatial procedure, legal costs and permit and environmental management. It is difficult to quote figures for these types of activities because they vary greatly from project to project. Wind turbines are also a source of revenue for the municipality. As with any construction project, the municipality collects so-called "construction fees" for the construction of wind turbines. These fees are one-off and, depending on the municipality, amount to about 1.5% of the construction sum. As mentioned, the municipality receives annual property taxes for wind turbines, on average 0.09% of the value of the turbine. The total municipal income via the property taxes for a 3 MW wind turbine over a period of 15 years, could then amount to over €40.000.[5]

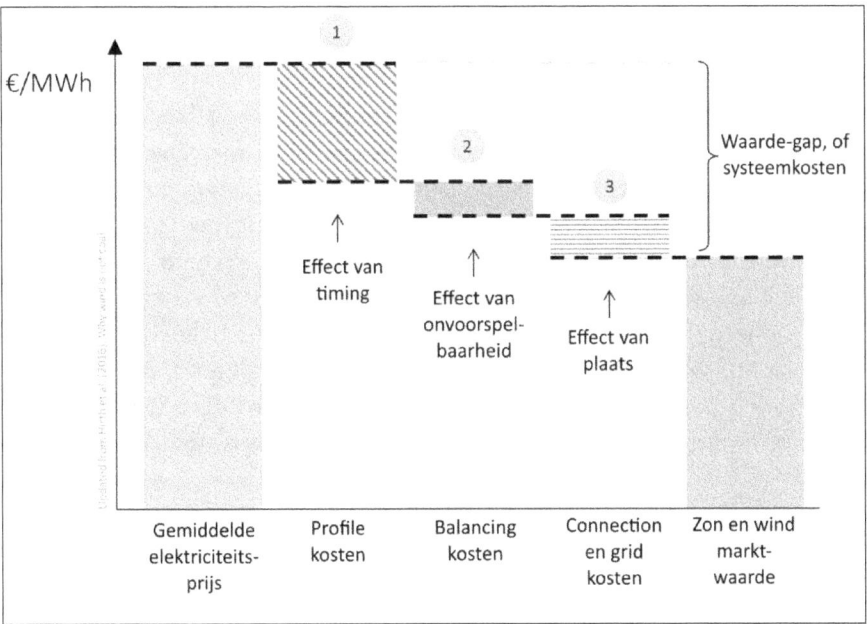

Fig. 5.1 Due to system costs, the value of solar and wind power is lower than average.[6]

System costs

Wind turbines generally have the advantage of no fuel costs. In addition, construction costs generally decrease with increasing production volumes. As a result, building wind turbines has become less expensive over the years. Since it is not only about cost, but also the value of the energy, construction costs do not say everything. Wind is unpredictable and can only generate energy part of the time anyway. This results in a lower energy value compared to traditional forms of energy. That lower value can be calculated by looking at the so-called system costs, the costs that must be incurred to fit the new energy source into the grid. These turn out to be substantial in the case of wind energy because of the high degree of variability and uncertainty. For this reason, many adjustments must be made in the grid to ensure the security of energy supply, including the following:
  - 'profile' costs - existing (fossil) power plants are increasingly taking on the function of backup in case the wind does not blow or the sun does not shine. As a result, those power plants can deliver much less favorably. These power plants can then only generate revenue part of the time, and during the time they do run, the efficiency decreases significantly due to the frequent switching on and off.
  - 'balancing' costs - because of the variability of wind, costs must be incurred to ensure stability of power supply.

- 'grid' and 'connection' costs - decentralized generation (especially offshore) requires companies such as Tennet and energy network companies to incur additional costs to make their grids suitable for it.

The decrease in the value of wind energy due to system costs is shown schematically in Figure 5.1.

In 2019, the Organization for Economic Cooperation and Development (OECD) conducted a comprehensive study of different scenarios for achieving the goals of the Paris climate agreement. This study shows that the system costs of variable renewable energy sources depend strongly on their share in the total energy supply. The costs increase more than proportionally with a larger share of solar and wind energy. This is shown in Figure 5.2, where the percentage of variable renewable energy (VRE) - energy generated by solar and wind - ranges from 10-30 and 50-75%. The 50% solar and wind scenario shows two variants: one where there is no exchange with neighboring countries - No IC, or no interconnections - but where energy storage in the form of hydro is possible and one where there is not - No IC, no flexible hydro.

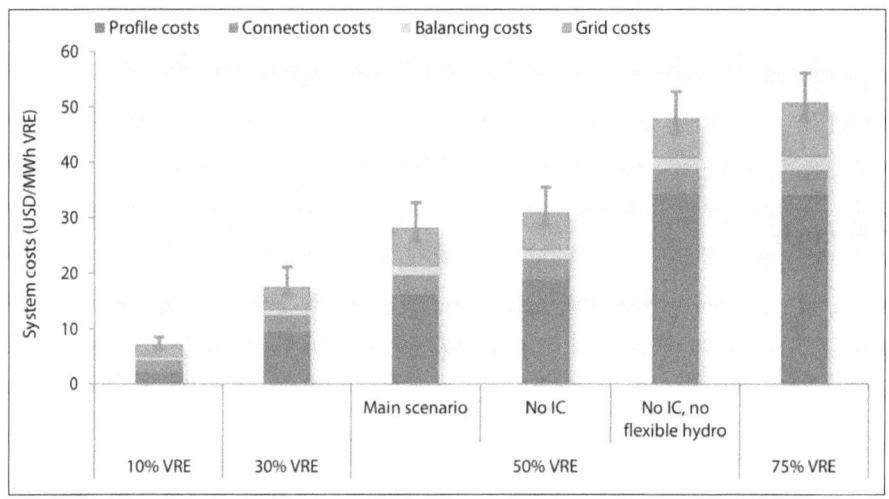

Fig. 5.2: System costs for variable renewables (VRE, solar and wind) increase sharply with their share in total energy supply.[7]

In general, system costs increase sharply with increasing shares of solar and wind power. In the case of 75% variable, this means almost a doubling of costs compared to the average (main) scenario. For the Netherlands it is also important to note that energy storage in the form of hydropower and/or reservoirs is not an issue, which means that even 50% solar and wind will lead to extra high costs anyway.

To compare the cost of wind and solar energy with other energy sources, the so-called Levelized Cost of Energy (LCOE) is used. This is the calculated cost of generating electricity per MegaWatt Hour (MWh) within the assumed lifetime of the renewable energy source. The total amount of electricity generated divided by all costs -

procurement, maintenance, fuel, financing, waste disposal, and so on - leads to the LCOE.

Proponents of wind and solar energy often arrive at a far too low LCOE by performing the calculation for a single wind or solar installation added to an existing grid. Similarly, Guido Bakema and Broer Scholten, in their 2016 book "Alles over Windenergie," are far too optimistic about the cost of generating 1MWh of wind energy compared to existing fossil fuels.[9] The Center of American Experiment's research shows that completely eliminating CO_2 emissions from energy supply will require large costs to remain assured of reliable supply at all times of the day. This involves large additional capacity and storage for the times when there is insufficient sun or wind.

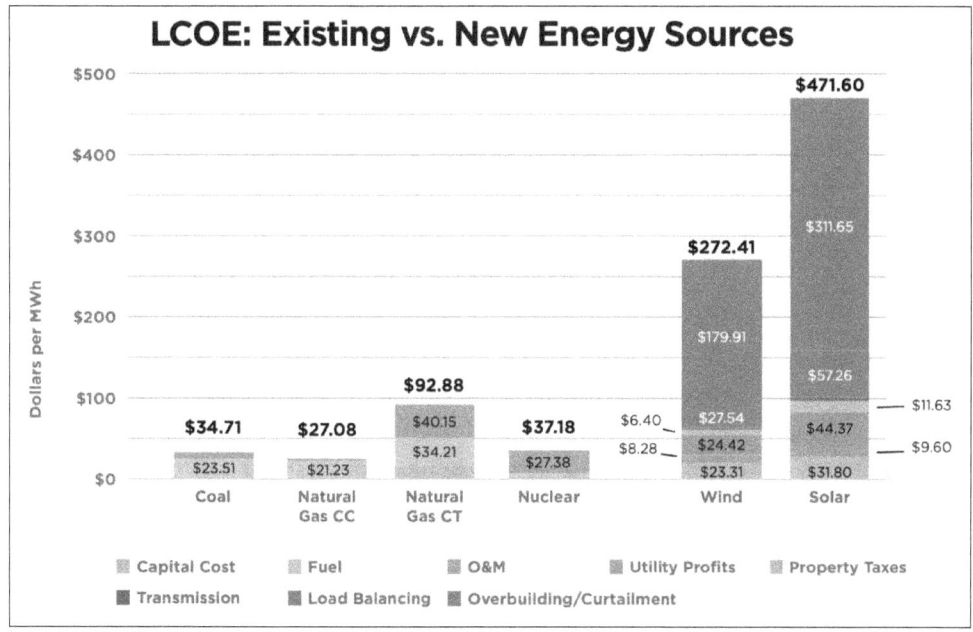

Fig. 5.3: On integral costing, solar and wind are found to be many times more expensive than traditional power plants.[8]

Figure 5.3 shows LCOE costs by energy type. Emergency excess capacity to accommodate periods of low wind and solar are the main reason for the high cost of wind and solar power. Solar and wind prove much more expensive per MWh than traditional (fossil) power plants when deployed on a large scale.

In the Netherlands, the exact cost of renewable energy is not clear. Nevertheless, we can get a good indication of the cost of solar and wind energy in the Netherlands if we compare it with other European countries. Figure 5.4 shows the total annual variable energy costs per household for each country. An average consumption per household of 2.770 kWh of electricity and 1.240 m3 of natural gas per year was assumed.[10] Price levels and data on installed capacity are from Eurostat and Wikipedia, respectively.[11][12] All figures refer to 2017, the latest year for which all data are available.

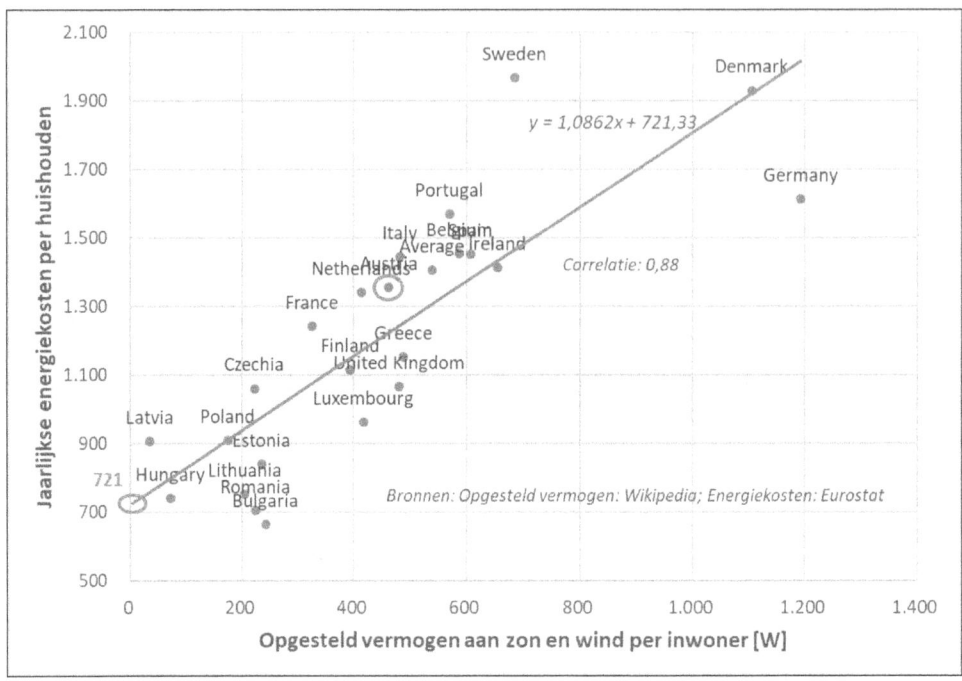

Fig. 5.4: Annual variable energy costs per household depend on the number of wind turbines and solar farms. Without solar and wind power, the cost per household in Europe averages €721.

Without energy based on solar and wind, the cost per household in Europe would average € 721 per year. In the Netherlands, variable energy costs in 2017 were €1341, or €620 more than needed. That means that with 7.8 million households in 2017, the combined annual cost was €4.8 billion higher than in the situation without renewable energy (€ 620 x 7.8 million = €4.8 billion).

According to the memorandum "National costs of energy transition in 2030" by the Netherlands Environmental Assessment Agency, the costs in 2030 are between €3.5-5.5 billion per year if 49% reduction of CO_2 is targeted.[13] These are the costs on top of those already incurred in the base path as outlined in the 2016 National Energy Outlook.[14] These are national costs - for Dutch society as a whole, regardless of who bears them - in the year 2030. The costs we are talking about here mainly concern subsidies for additional deployment of renewable energy, storage of CO_2, reduction of energy demand, heat networks, etc. But also, for example, the increase in the cost price of fuel by blending biofuel with fossil fuel. With the above information, it becomes clear that this will rather add up to a multiple of this amount.

The figures cited here refer to 2017. The share of energy generated by solar and wind in total electricity generation in that year was 13%. With the passage of the Climate Act in 2019, the rollout of solar and wind has gained momentum. The costs of wind turbines and solar panels have declined slightly, a trend that is likely to continue, especially for solar panels, but that does not outweigh the system costs mentioned above that will increase more than proportionately and the declining yields per megawatt of installed capacity with a greater share of solar and wind power. Therefore, there is no argument that the correlation shown will become much more favorable in coming years.

This means that if the share of solar and wind increases from 13% in 2017 to, say, 50% in 2030, the annual additional cost of power generation will be 3 to 4 times higher than €4.8 billion, i.e., in the order of €15 to €19 billion per year. This corresponds to €1850 to €2350 per household per year, based on 8.1 million households in 2022. This annual amount may only be lower if there is a technical breakthrough in which wind turbines, for example, provide energy a greater proportion of the time, or an inexpensive and efficient way to store wind energy is developed. Indications of that, however, are not yet available.

Unforeseen costs

In addition to the costs discussed above, unforeseen costs often crop up during the construction, installation, and operation of wind turbines. This can sometimes be a major setback for companies involved in wind energy. Wind turbine manufacturers depend on market prices of raw materials and energy, among other things, in addition to rising personnel costs.

For example, the cost of installing wind turbines can add up significantly if the various phases of construction are not well matched. During operation, unexpected quality problems can lead to necessary maintenance or the need to replace parts. With the explosive increase in the number of onshore and offshore wind turbines, several aspects are increasingly determining the profitability of companies in the wind energy sector.

Energy revenues and subsidization

One would almost forget with all these costs that there is also energy revenue, something investors are all about. However, it is not easy to determine exactly how much wind turbine operators get for their electricity. It depends on which market they sell their electricity in. When calculating revenues, the market price for electricity and the number of hours a wind turbine is effectively running are important. Electricity from wind turbines yields less than electricity from other energy sources, such as gas power plants. There are several reasons for this. First, not the same amount of wind energy is produced at every moment, simply because the wind does not always blow at the same speed. Moreover, wind turbines generate relatively much electricity during windy nights when there is less consumption. That, too, depresses the price. All this leads to electricity from wind turbines yielding about 11% less than the average market price, which is determined by the ratio of available energy resources (supply) to energy consumption (demand).

The number of hours the turbine effectively runs is also important. In industry jargon, this is called "full-load hours". By this is meant the length of time the energy source has effectively produced energy at full power. Wind turbines do not always run at full power and therefore do not produce the maximum amount of energy all the time. It is therefore important to look at these full-load hours, as they are normative for energy yields.

Siemens Energy

German energy company Siemens Energy disclosed in January 2023 that it expects to post another loss in the 2023 fiscal year. This is mainly due to ongoing problems at its Spanish wind turbine subsidiary Siemens Gamesa. That company is struggling with supply problems, quality problems of its own products, rising raw material costs and an increasing regulatory burden for the installation of onshore wind turbines. Although rising raw material costs and increasing regulatory pressure also apply to other wind turbine manufacturers, they are showing better numbers. Siemens Gamesa has unspecified design issues and quality problems with bearings and rotor blades, specifically with the latest wind turbine models.

Siemens Energy, in publishing preliminary results for the first quarter of fiscal year 2023, warned that its net loss this year will be around last year's level. In fiscal year 2022, the company suffered a loss of 647 million euros. This would put the group in the red for the fourth year in a row.[15]

Siemens Gamesa said it made a preliminary loss before interest and taxes of about 760 million euros in the first quarter. The turbine maker faced a significant setback of 472 million euros in the first quarter of 2023, as technical shortfalls were discovered during an inspection of installed wind turbines that resulted in higher-than-expected warranty and maintenance costs.

Siemens Energy took full control of the Spanish subsidiary in 2022 and has since taken a 93 percent stake. Last year, Siemens Gamesa also replaced its top executive after a series of profit warnings.

The revenues of a wind turbine can ultimately be calculated by multiplying the number of full-load hours by the power in kilowatts of the wind turbine. This total multiplied by the price per kWh paid by the customer on the *futures market* determines the revenues for the operator per year. A 3 MW wind turbine - or 3000 kW - on land with 2000 full-load hours and a sales rate (NB no consumer price of €0.23 and not counting negative prices) of €0.04 per kWh yields 3000 x 2000 x 0.04 euros per year. That is an annual amount of € 240.000.

In addition to these revenues, the operator of a wind farm is eligible for government subsidies.[16] Through this subsidy scheme (In the Netherlands SDE++), the difference between the cost price of the technology - the "base amount" - and the average market remuneration for the energy generated is reimbursed to the operator for up to 15 years. In practice, the subsidy amounts to about 2 to 3 cents per kWh of energy generated. For the same 3 MW wind turbine as in the example above, this means an annual additional output of 3000 x 2000 x 0.03 euros per year. This is an annual subsidy of €180.000.

Decreasing wind strength

The energy output of a wind turbine depends on the amount of wind. However, several measured wind strength data over the years show that the average wind has been decreasing over the past 30 years.[17][18] While it is true that there are locations where higher wind strengths have been measured, at most measured locations the measurements show decreasing wind strength. This decreasing wind strength trend seems to be continuing. This is extremely unfavorable for the total power to be generated by wind turbines, since wind speed is the most important factor for yield, as discussed in Chapter 2.

CBS, a Dutch governmental organization, uses a wind index, or wind index (Windex-CBS), derived from wind turbine production data for its analyses. This measure gives the monthly or annual electricity production relative to the long-term average, independent of the installed capacity. The low values of this Windex-CBS fit very well into the picture of the declining trend of about 1% per year that has been observed for over three decades. Dutch wind measurements indicate increasingly calm wind conditions. Figure 5.5 shows the wind index over the period 1988-2010, noting that the method of calculating the wind index has changed twice. Until 1995, the index was derived from wind measurements. From 1996 through 2008, the index was based on yields from about 60 wind turbines, and from 2009, CBS calculates the index from the yields of many wind farms in the Netherlands.[19]

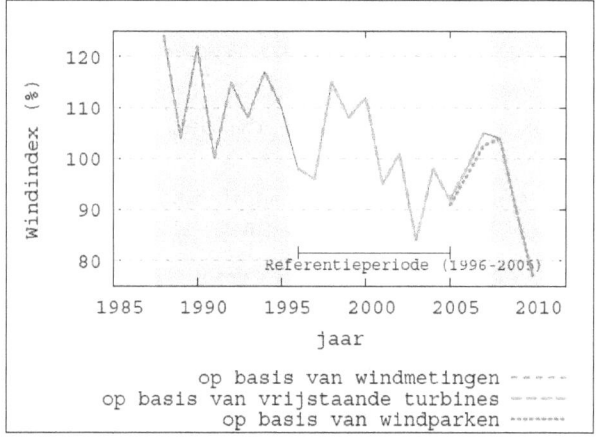

Fig. 5.5: The so-called wind index in the period 1988 - 2010. In it, the decreasing wind strength can be observed.

Incidentally, the decrease in wind is a phenomenon not only observed in the Netherlands. Decreases in wind are observed throughout the northern hemisphere, as Figure 5.6 shows.[20] Measurements between 1979-2008 show that average wind speed decreased by between 5-15% during that period. In Central Asia, it even decreased by about 20%. Most monitoring stations measure wind speed at 10 meters altitude. While the unfavorable trend measured at 10 meters is less pronounced at 50-100 meters altitude, the reduced wind supply can still make just the difference between profitability or not. So, for the wind turbine industry, these kinds of measurements are crucial. The trend in the decrease in wind speed started back in the 1960s. As

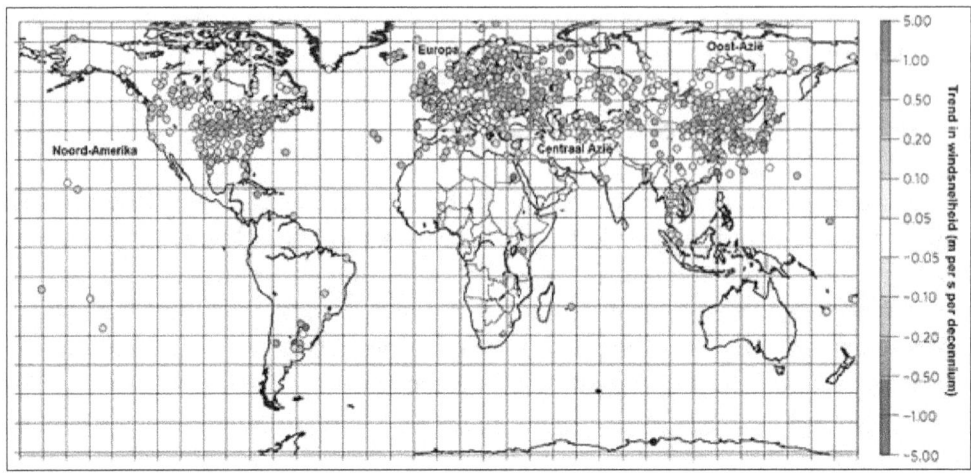

Fig. 5.6: Decrease in wind speed in m/s, by decade, measured between 1979 and 2008.[21]

measurements have shown, this declining trend has continued from 2008 to the present.

The impact of wind strength on the amount of energy generated in a year becomes clear when years with high and low wind are compared. In the winter of 2022/'23, 12% less energy was generated by wind turbines in absolute terms in the Netherlands than in the winter of the previous year. And this despite the increase in the number of wind turbines. The lack of wind with a strength between 6-9 Bft played a major role in this.[22][23] After all, the maximum power of a wind turbine is generated at wind force 6 as described in Chapter 2. Above wind force 9, the turbines are only shut down.

Since the generating capacity of a wind turbine is proportional to the speed to the third power (as explained in Chapter 2), the decrease in wind strength has a very large effect on the total calculated yield from wind in the northern hemisphere. With further wind decline, theoretically predicted yields from wind farms will not be met, and this means that the cost-to-benefit ratio for wind power will be higher at the same kWh price. Wind farm investors do not like to see their projected profits evaporate and so the price will once again have to be paid by the consumer.

Trust or distrust

When companies or wealthy individuals claim their assets in a bank, it can lead to a bank failure. In the first months of 2023, a number of banks collapsed, including Silicon Valley Bank in California and Credit Suisse in Switzerland.

A quote from Sander Boon in an article in "Gezond Verstand" magazine captures the shaky basis of trust: "Trust in the economy must remain high, because the financial system exists by the grace of the trust we have in it. Indeed, our prosperity exists largely on paper; it is the promise that we will pay off our debts from future economic growth."[24]

Contribution to economic growth

The construction, installation and operation of wind turbines is an increasingly important contributor to global economic growth. More and more products and services in the wind market are contributing to it. However, the prevailing model of global economic growth is creating more and more debt. Wind trade is also driven by debt and thus has a shaky foundation of trust, see box.

Wind farm investors

Financing of wind farms is mostly done by commercial banks, financial institutions, hedge fund, export credit insurers - supported by the government - and energy companies. In addition, wind farms are also financed by pension funds, with Dutch pension fund ABP's share being remarkably large. ABP announced in December 2022 that it will invest 30 billion euros in the energy transition, with a particular focus on investments in large-scale wind farms in the North Sea. The investment of those 30 billion Euros is planned until 2030.[25] Another pension fund, the Physiotherapists Pension Fund Foundation (SPF) invested in one of the world's largest onshore wind farms in Sweden, called Markbygden Wind Farm. Investments by pension funds are made under the rubric of the UN's Sustainable Development Goals.[26]

A total of 96 banks in Europe are active in financing wind energy in 2021. Dutch banks ING Group and Rabobank rank third and seventh, respectively, with percentages of 4.3% and 3.2% of total bank financing.[1]

A second form of financing takes place from the equity of large energy companies and grid operators. Energy companies and grid operators ask their shareholders to increase the company's equity through financial contributions to invest in the construction of - and networks for - wind farms. One example is grid operator Liander. In mid-2021, shareholders were asked for a financial contribution of €600 million to invest in energy transition. Discussions are also being held with the Consumer & Market Authority and the Ministries of Finance and Economic Affairs and Climate on possible solutions to the financing challenges within the energy sector. Liander, responsible for the grid connection of some three million households in the Netherlands, has been investing around 1.2 billion euros a year since 2021 to reinforce the networks to connect wind and solar farms to the grid. This is double the investment compared to previous years. [27]

Carbon credits

In addition to huge amounts of money being invested in the realization of wind turbines and the infrastructure required to do so, there is also a large money flow surrounding the trade in so-called carbon credits. A carbon credit is a tradable certificate that states that somewhere in the world a ton of carbon dioxide will be removed from the air. Whoever buys such a certificate may emit a ton of CO_2 themselves and then call themselves "climate neutral". This offers financial and strategic advantages, and so companies are willing to pay for it. A carbon credit is a security, just like banknotes, bonds, and shares. Legally, however, there are important differences. The issuance of securities is normally subject to strict rules. For example, you cannot just issue bonds: that requires specialized financial institutions. For carbon credits, however, no such rules exist.

CO_2 emissions offset on paper have become one of the goals of wind farms. The emissions avoided on paper have become a form of credit. With enough "carbon credits," companies that are imposed a CO_2 reduction target - for example, the mandatory 55% CO_2 reduction by 2030 - can buy off their own CO_2 emissions, which benefits the wind farm investor.

It works like this. Companies subjected to CO_2 reduction requirements enlist the help of an investment company. The latter then invests the money paid by the company (and various subsidies from governments) in the construction of wind farms.

Investment companies today are also often engaged by consulting firms. These, in turn, help companies draw up a plan on how to achieve the required objectives. The explosive growth of this type of consulting firm already indicates that this has created an extremely lucrative business model. In fact, companies cannot do otherwise. Since they have their hands full with their own business operations, they usually have neither the quality nor the capacity to respond to this kind of sweeping regulation from the government.

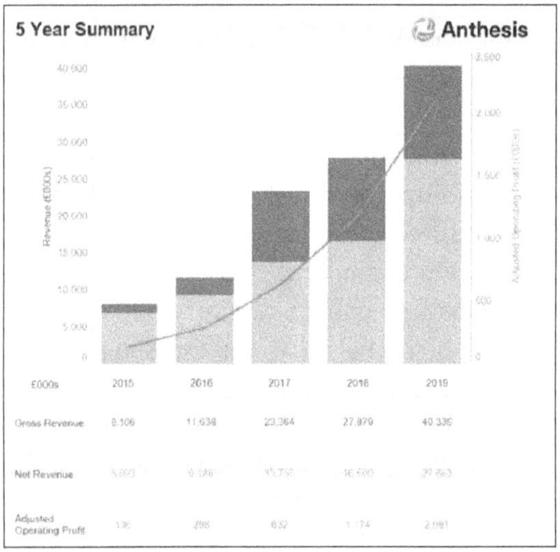

The company Anthesis is one such carbon credit trading consultancy. A group of consultants that supports the Sustainable Development Goals and advises companies on how to reduce CO_2 emissions. Figure 5.7 shows Anthesis' growth. Anthesis' full-service Net Zero offerings include services such as CO_2 reduction strategies, provision of high-value offsets, technological innovations, extensive project development capabilities and certification.

Fig. 5.7: Growth of Consultancy firm Anthesis as per 2019 annual report in picture, [28] typical of the explosive growth of similar firms that are thriving on carbon trading.

An example of a CO_2 offset project is South Africa's first AgriCarbon program. This project rewards farmers using carbon credits they can "earn" through supposedly sustainable farming practices. Such projects contribute to the United Nations' goals - the SDGs. Anthesis helps more than 2.600 clients around the world reduce CO_2 emissions. One of Anthesis' ambitions is to reduce three gigatons of CO_2 for clients by 2030.

Another ambition of Anthesis, as one of the fastest-growing private companies in the UK and Europe, is to build on its position as a market leader and talent pool for sustainability professionals by 2022.

Agencies like Anthesis, which thrive on the exponential growth of carbon trading, do not always deliver on their promises. This became clear recently from a publication by investigative journalism platform *Follow The Money*.[29] The company South Pole sells carbon credits, which companies can use to neutralize their greenhouse gas emissions. FTM showed that South Pole's main CO_2-compensation project yielded far fewer climate gains than the company claimed.

Over 60% of the carbon credits South Pole created with the Kariba Forest project in Zimbabwe were realized only on paper, according to internal analyses. Thus, 27 million tons of CO_2 - comparable to seven times the annual emissions of all of Amsterdam - were never offset but largely released into the air. That makes the climate performance of customers who bought the deliberate CO_2 allowances largely worthless. Even after South Pole discovered in the summer of 2022 that it had made a gross mistake, it continued to sell emissions allowances to major clients, including consulting firms McKinsey and EY.

So, the successes South Pole celebrated in recent years are partly based on thin air. This was discovered by Follow the Money in early 2023. For years, South Pole sold fictitious emission rights to hundreds of companies, including Gucci, energy supplier Greenchoice and consulting firms McKinsey and EY mentioned earlier. Follow the Money's article appeared shortly after similar publications by British newspaper The Guardian and German newspaper Die Zeit. They showed, based on scientific studies, that possibly more than 90% of all CO_2 offsets coming from forest projects in the tropics are flawed.[30]

But not only in Europe is this kind of issue at play. Also, in America and Canada, several nature reserves with protected status have been bought up by investors as "protected nature reserves." These vast forests guarantee a large number of carbon credits as they guarantee years of absorption of CO_2 from the air. Meanwhile, numerous cases have become public where it turned out that after trading the carbon credits of the "nature reserve," the forests were still cut down and the trees burned in large biomass plants. So, of the presented CO_2 uptake that was traded in exchange for the carbon credits, nothing remains in the end ... except much, much capital for the consulting firms and the investor in the reserve.

Understanding climate spending

Governments, including in the Netherlands, are now spending billions on "climate policy. These expenditures must be accounted for by these same governments. However, it has turned out that large amounts cannot be traced. In the Netherlands, the General Audit Office (GAO) audits the income and expenditure of the central government and reports to parliament in the annual Accountability Survey. The GAO also investigates the costs and effects of government policies. On January 25, 2023, the

GAO sent a letter to the president of the House of Representatives, which noted several striking issues. First, the various overviews of climate spending differ from one another. Second, climate expenditures are not recorded unambiguously by ministries. Third, there is a lack of definitions of what can be counted as climate expenditure. Finally, it concluded that climate expenditures remain out of sight and that some expenditures may be mistaken as climate expenditures. The result, the GAO argued, is that the House of Representatives does not get a consistent picture of Dutch climate spending.[31]

According to the Climate Memorandum, the government is spending €4 to €6.9 billion annually on climate policy measures in the period to 2030. Those measures aim to reduce CO_2 emissions. The spending includes measures related to electricity, industry and circular economy, agriculture, housing, and mobility. These include subsidy schemes for the purchase of a heat pump or an electric car. The fluctuations in planned spending are related to the temporary nature of certain measures. For example, around 2025 there are more subsidy schemes for purchasing a heat pump. With the planned establishment of a €35 billion Climate Fund, annual climate spending could double in the period up to 2030. In the context of this great financial importance, it is remarkable how the House of Representatives has been given insight into climate spending in recent years.

Substantial amounts of climate spending cannot be traced, such as spending on connecting offshore wind farms. The Minister of Finance writes in the 2022 Budget Memorandum that connecting offshore wind farms will cost €150 million less than what the Minister of Economic Affairs states in his budget. Apparently, the high priority of climate policy does not mean that citizens' tax money needs to be handled carefully.

Impact of wind energy on the power grid

Since power from wind farms is given priority on the power grid, conventional fossil-fuel power plants (coal, natural gas) must continuously ramp up and down depending on wind power. This significantly lowers the efficiency and environmental performance of conventional power plants.
When there is little wind, wind farms provide little or no power, and conventional power plants must meet the total demand for energy. Thus, to avoid blackouts, it is necessary to keep the full power capacity supplied by classic power plants operational. So, there is no other option than to keep two complete energy systems, classical and renewable, operational at the same time.[33]

The Dutch system operator TenneT, which is responsible for the security of electricity supply and demand and supply on the grid, must balance what is known as the energy balance. TenneT is fully owned by the Ministry of Finance and thus the Dutch government. TenneT is a monopolist and alone manages the Dutch grid of 110 kV and above.

> **Negative energy prices**
>
> If wind farms supply more power than demand at times of high wind, this results in the need to shut down wind turbines and/or supply energy at a negative price. A number of times this has already occurred in The Netherlands, for example on April 23, 2022 when at the peak of the day the supply of energy was 20% higher than the demand. This was caused by the fact that it was sunny that day combined with a lot of wind. As a result, the energy price reached -0.18 euros per kilowatt hour.[32] When this happens, energy producers are charging money and they are not receiving subsidies. The more wind farms, the more often this will happen and the higher the average electricity price for consumers can be. In fact, a negative power price means that households with solar panels and a dynamic contract at that time have to charge money to be allowed to feed their generated solar energy into the grid.
>
> Negative prices are more common. In all of 2022, there were 100 hours of negative prices. This number had already reached May 31 this year. Besides wind, solar is a culprit. For 2023, 250 hours of negative prices are expected in The Netherlands.

TenneT warned in January 2023 of a power shortage in 2030.[34] In a report for the Ministry of Economic Affairs, TenneT wrote that power generation shortages could occur in seven years. As a result, the desired electricity demand may not be fully met at all hours of the year. Internationally, the security of electricity supply in the Netherlands is currently extremely high at 99.99963 percent.[33] However, TenneT sees this changingand that has everything to do with the increasing demand for power with, at the same time, increasing dependence on the weather. Despite this truth-warning from the grid operator, environmental activist organizations such as the Dutch "Natuur & Milieu" continue to advocate closing all coal-fired power plants by 2025.

TenneT, as an electricity specialist, has long known that we cannot phase out stable power supplies such as nuclear and coal power plants without consequences, while at the same time building up unstable power supplies (wind and solar) and also rapidly creating more power purchases. Environmental organizations know this too because they have access to the same information. As early as 2022, it became clear that power shortages were imminent in several provinces in the Netherlands. On June 8, 2022, for example, it was reported that in Brabant and Limburg the high-voltage grid was full and no new companies could be connected to the electricity grid.[35] Incidentally, this puts the Netherlands in the company of Switzerland, France and Germany, among others.

The reliability of the current network

Our social dependence on electricity is only increasing due to ever-increasing digitalization and developments within the energy transition. After all, the objectives in the climate agreement must be pursued, leading to a shift from fossil to renewable energy sources. These further increases both the demand for electricity and the interconnectedness of various players within the energy supply. As both dependence on and pressure on electricity supply increase, electricity outages will have major effects. Chapter 3 (the consequences of Dutch climate policy) gives examples of climate obligations that will lead to a higher load on the electricity network.

The electricity grid is also becoming more complex. Partly due to the energy transition, challenges arise for the stability of the electricity network, which is such an essential facility for a modern society, such as the Dutch one, that failure can lead to serious social disruption. This makes it a threat to national security, as noted in the National Electricity Crisis Plan issued by the Ministry of Economic Affairs and Climate in 2021.[36]

Blackouts hardly ever occur in the Dutch power grid at present, and electric driving does not yet have to be curtailed, as it might be in Switzerland. There, a legislative bill was introduced in December 2022 that could ban the use of electric cars in winter in case there is a shortage of electricity.[37][38] Switzerland can generate satisfactory energy in the summer thanks to hydroelectric plants. In winter, however, the country relies largely on electricity imports, particularly from France and Germany. In 2021, that was 5.7 billion kilowatt hours.

Since France and Germany are also currently dealing with unstable electricity production - France frequently suffers from the failure of nuclear power plants, Germany relies largely on unpredictable power from wind and solar energy - Switzerland today has to reckon with a high risk of power outages. This also shows that the electricity grid is not made for the large fluctuations of renewable energy and for higher power consumption from electrical process industry, heating and automobility.

TenneT could and should have expanded its own grid in response to the 10-year grid development plan presented by the EU back in 2012.[39] This, based on the political ambitions for changes in electricity production and consumption. However, this did not happen. TenneT did publish investment plans for "onshore grid" and "offshore grid" in 2022 for the period from 2022 – 2031 though. Figure 5.8 shows these graphically.[40] Altogether, they amount to tens of billions of euros in investments for the next 10 years.

Those required expansions take a long time, especially due to land use planning procedures. As a result, a temporary mismatch between grid expansion and capacity demand could not be avoided. This mismatch is compounded by a chronic shortage of technicians and the organization and lead time required to educate and train new employees at TenneT.

But grid expansion is not the grid operator's only challenge. A significant portion of the 110kV and 150 kV substations have reached the end of their service life. Over one hundred high-voltage substations must be replaced in the coming years. This is a serious challenge and requires a lot of commitment of money and resources to ensure that security of supply is guaranteed in the future as well.

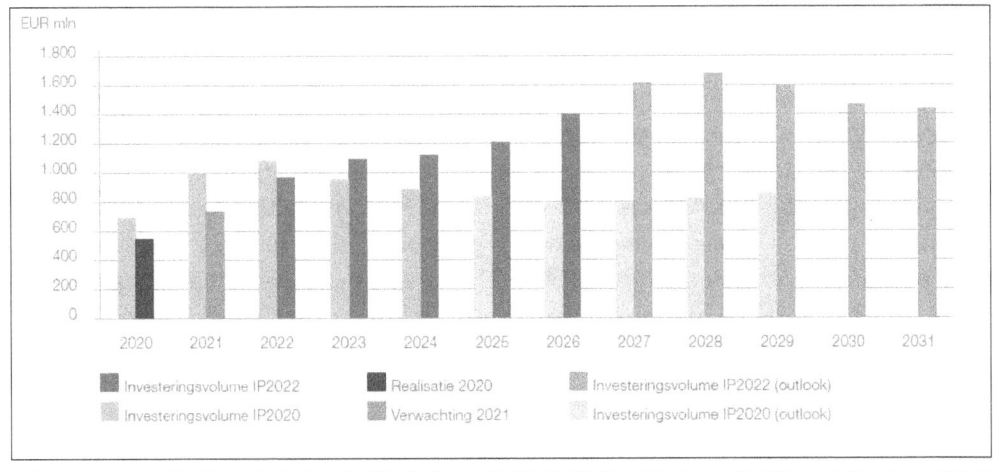

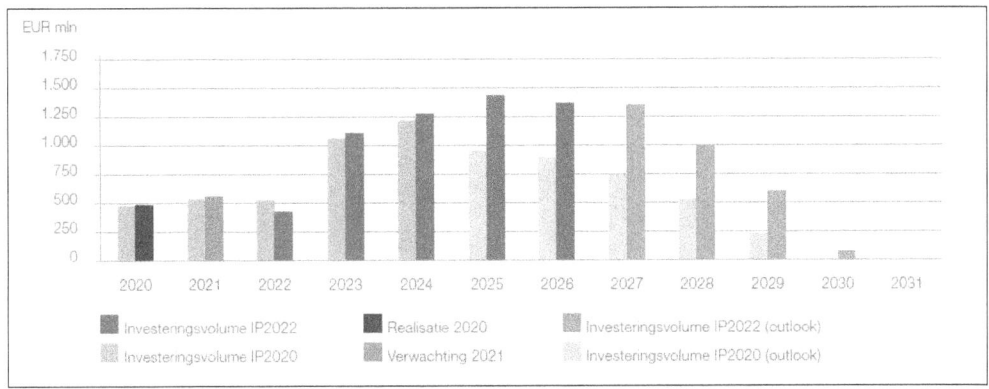

Fig. 5.8: TenneT investment plan for increasing grid capacity.
Plan for 'onshore grid' above and plan for 'offshore grid' below.

TenneT is currently swamped with work. There is far more work than the company can handle, which is why TenneT has to set priorities. Because this involves societal interests, the national and regional governments are consulting with the grid operators to set priorities at the national and regional levels. The choice of what will and will not be tackled in the short term, inevitably means that various bottlenecks will not be resolved until (much) later than they would have been if sufficient manpower and resources had been available. TenneT also has to deal with processing times for permit applications and possible public participation procedures. The dependence on these further complicates the planning of activities and can lead to unforeseen delays.

The fact that priorities are not always set correctly by grid operators was demonstrated by the fact that a solar field with 5.500 panels in Barendrecht, officially opened in September 2022, had been ready for months but could not be connected to the electricity grid.[41] The outcry about this was great: this cannot be explained to the taxpayer who, left or right, always pays for the costs.

What all this means for your wallet

By now it will have become clear that a great deal of money is involved in the wind turbine industry and the wind trade created around it. As consumers' energy bills continue to rise, the large energy corporations, sponsored by banks and investment companies, see their profits soar to exorbitant levels. In addition, under the guise of climate change, all kinds of taxes are being introduced or raised to implement the climate agenda. A distressing example is the recent increase in the airline tax by a whopping 332%.[42] The energy tax was also sharply increased by the government on January 1, 2023 to €0.59 per m³ gas, and €0.15 per kWh electricity.[43] The increasing costs of the necessary infrastructure and the high system costs of wind power, while borne by the government, must be paid by taxpayers.

It has also become clear that a substantial portion of taxpayers' pension money is being invested in wind farms, farms where it is clear in advance that they can never become profitable to contribute to pension fund returns. Pension security is thus totally undermined by the implementation of the climate agenda. Every year, billions of pension money disappears into the pockets of stakeholders other than pension beneficiaries.

1. Report "Financing and investment trends," The European wind industry in 2021, www.windeurope.org
2. www.mo.be/analyse/windturbines-vlaanderen-hoeveel-kosten-ze-en-hoeveel-leveren-ze-op
3. www.irena.org/publications/2020/Jun/Renewable-Power-Costs-in-2019
4. www.vastelastenbond.nl/energie/windenergie-alles-over-windmolens-in-nederland/
5. www.rvo.nl/onderwerpen/windenergie-op-land/subsidies-en-financiering
6 (PDF) Market value and the future of renewables, Lion Hirth, November 2015; energiforskmedia.blob.core.windows.net/media/21039/3_neon-energy_hirth.pdf
7. Nuclear Energy Agency (NEA) - Executive Summary of The Costs of Decarbonization: System Costs with High Shares of Nuclear and Renewables; www.oecd-nea.org
8.(PDF) The-High-Cost-of-100-Percent-Carbon-Free-Electricity-by-2040-in-Minnesota.pdf; www.americanexperiment.org.
9. Book "All about Wind Energy"; Guido Bakema and Broer Scholten, 2016
10. www.tno.nl/en/about-tno/organisation/units/energy-transition/
11. en.wikipedia.org/wiki/Wind_power_in_the_European_Union
12. ec.europa.eu/eurostat/statistics-explained/index.php?title=Electricity_price_statistics
13. www.pbl.nl/publicaties/nationale-kosten-energietransitie-in-2030
14. www.pbl.nl/en/publications/national-energy-outlook-2016
15. www.deondernemer.nl/actueel/siemens-energy-verwacht-verlies-door-problemen-windturbines~4330915?referrer=https%3A%2F%2Fwww.google.com%2F
16. www.rvo.nl/subsidies-financiering/sde/werking
17. www.knmi.nl/over-het-knmi/nieuws/het-waait-minder-hard-in-nederland
18. www.cbs.nl/en-gb/

19. Article "Decomposition of the windiness index in The Netherlands for the assessment of future long-term wind supply"; Wind Energy Volume 16, issue 6, Sep 2013, p 811 - 975
20. www.nrc.nl/nieuws/2010/10/19/het-waait-steeds-minder-11958849-a756681
21. www.nature.com/articles/ngeo979
22. www.zonneplan.nl/blog/12-procent-minder-wind-en-zonne-energie-winter-2023
23. www.weer.nl/nieuws/2023/geen-stormen-en-stormnamen-ongebruikt-hoe-kan-dat
24. gezondverstand.eu/2023/02/13/nummer-59-18-feb-2023/#nummer-59-18-feb-2023/16/
25. wind-energy-news.co.uk/16/pension-fund-abp-announces-tightened-climate-policy//
26. Documentary Headwind "21 by documentary filmmaker Marijn Poels; www.youtube.com/watch?v=7RgyLDVlAg4
27. www.alliander.com/nl/nieuws/aandeelhouders-doen-investering-in-de-energietransitie/
28. www.annualreports.com/Company/anthesis-group
29. www.ftm.nl/artikelen/pijnlijke-feiten-verdienmodel-south-pole
30. www.theguardian.com/environment/2023/jan/18/revealed-forest-carbon-offsets-biggest-provider-worthless-verra-aoe
31. www.rekenkamer.nl/onderwerpen/klimaat-energie-en-milieu/nieuws/2023/01/25/kamer-krijgt-geen-totaalplaatje-klimaatuitgaven
32. solarplan.news/press-releases/Saturday-23-April-for-the-first-time-free-power
33. www.wyniasweek.nl/stroomtekort-wacht-dan-met-van-het-gas-af-gaan-en-met-elektrisch-rijden/
34. nos.nl/article/2459559-network operator-warns-of-power-shortage-in-2030
35. www.omroepbrabant.nl/nieuws/4098821/hoogspanningsnet-zit-vol-geen-aansluitingen-meer-voor-nieuwe-bedrijven
(PDF) National Electricity Crisis Plan, Ministry of Economic Affairs and Climate; public document 36.
37. www.newsd.admin.ch/newsd/message/attachments/74051.pdf
38. www.blckbx.tv/buitenland/zwitserland-kan-bij-stroomtekort-rijverbod-invoeren-voor-elektrische-autos
39. eur-lex.europa.eu/legal-content/NL/TXT/PDF/?uri=CELEX:32012L0027&from=HR
40. www.tennet.eu/home
41. www.rijnmond.nl/nieuws/1552208/zonneveld-met-5500-panelen-vangt-al-maanden-zon-maar-kabels-naar-het-stroomnet-zijn-nog-steeds-niet-gelegd
42. www.rijksoverheid.nl/onderwerpen/belastingplan/klimaat/vliegbelasting.
43. www.milieucentraal.nl/energie-besparen/inzicht-in-je-energierekening/energiebelasting-2023/

Fig. 5.9: The "lone cyclist" no longer has his gaze on the horizon, but on a row of wind turbines.

Chapter 6: The effects of wind turbines on people and nature

Finally, after all the perils outlined above, we must also discuss the impact of the large-scale wind industry on people and nature. Individual wind turbines and wind farms dramatically change the view of the landscape. In addition, the construction, production, but also the use of wind turbines has an enormous impact on people and nature. This concerns the entire cycle: from the extraction of all necessary raw materials to the dismantling and removal of the wind turbine. Even after that, a wind turbine currently causes damage to the environment; especially the rotor blade which is made of fiberglass reinforced epoxy and for which no recycling method has yet been developed.

To limit the impact of wind turbines on people and nature, requirements and guidelines are set by governments for the construction and operation of wind turbines. These guidelines and requirements are also used by the same government to justify their construction. However, these guidelines and requirements are often not or poorly substantiated, as I will demonstrate with several examples in this chapter.

As we saw, the world is on the eve of an explosion in the number of wind turbines. Not to mention their removal. Reports of new wind farms in the North Sea, totaling as many as 30.000 wind turbines, make that more than clear.[1] It is, therefore, of the utmost importance to further investigate the harmful effects on people and nature. Indeed, the environmental impact assessment on which the granting of a permit for the construction of one or more wind turbines is based must take all harmful effects into account.

The best-known adverse effects of wind turbines are the dropshadow, the production of low-frequency noise and the number of bird, bat and insect casualties they cause. However, there are many other adverse effects, such as the use of the harmful gas SF6 for electrical insulation in wind turbines, which is not even considered in current environmental impact studies. Here are some little-named harmful effects.

Forest damage

To meet citizen demands to place wind turbines as far away from civilization as possible, sparsely populated areas are often sought. Usually these are larger forest areas. In countless places around the world, entire forests are cut down to make way for wind turbines, even though it is precisely the trees that effectively remove CO_2 from the air and convert it into biomass and the oxygen needed for life.

Germany is one of the countries that generates the most wind energy. Wind turbines have become real eye-catchers in the landscape there. Germany, traditionally a large country with ancient forests, is effortlessly sacrificing them for wind farms. The Reinhardswald in Germany, for example, is also suffering. At 20.000 hectares, the

Reinhardswald is the largest contiguous forest area in the state of Hessen. Parts of the forest have now been cleared to install twenty 240-meter-high wind turbines there. This forest near Kassel is a so-called "primeval forest" with ancient oaks. The forest inspired the Brothers Grimm when writing their fairy tales. Germany has several such primeval forests, colloquially called Hudewälder, forests in which locals favored oak over beech growth for pigs and other livestock. In the name of climate protection, cutting down trees in these primeval forests is allowed by the German government. By the way, the term "sustainability" (Nachhaltigkeit) was invented three centuries ago in German forestry. Back then it meant "not harvesting more than you need and adjusting your planting plan accordingly".[2]

Fig. 6.1: Building the Markbygden windpark in Sweden.[4]

To somewhat dampen the spirits of the regional population and minimize resistance, the government distributes flyers giving reasons for cutting down the forest. One of the reasons for building wind turbines exactly there is that the wind turbines "will not be in the primeval forest, but in fast-growing pine forest that was destroyed by a storm (Friederike) in 2018 anyway". It is also argued that the bark beetle has severely damaged the trees in the forest. But the main argument to justify cutting down primeval forest is that the wind farm that will replace it, will provide energy for many thousands of households. Although this provides some support among the population, resistance is growing. For the romantically inclined Germans, the forest has a symbolic value. Destroying the fairytale forest can thus also be seen as indigenous cultural destruction. Attempts to stop the cutting of trees, however, get bogged down in complicated and drawn-out legal procedures.

But not only German nature has to suffer. In Sweden, too, entire forests are being sacrificed to wind turbines. In his 2021 documentary Headwind, documentary filmmaker Marijn Poels depicts the construction of Markbygden, one of the world's largest onshore wind farms in Sweden.[3] The documentary reveals how large areas of forest have been destroyed to make way for large wind turbines in Sweden's remote and vast forests. By the way, not only for the wind turbine itself. First, in fact, roads are being paved for the supply of heavy construction equipment. A lot of forest must already be cut down for this purpose. At the locations where the wind turbines will be placed, after the trees have been removed, explosives are used to blow up the rocky subsoil. This is necessary for the foundations of the wind turbines.

A salient detail is that much of the energy generated at the Markbygden wind farm is used by a Google data center in Finland.

In addition to the damage to forests caused by the installation of wind turbines, Ecuador, the country with the largest market share of balsa wood (i.e., 75% of the world trade), is illegally cutting down balsa trees in the Amazon.[5] More recent wind turbine designs have blades as long as 100 meters, each of which consumes about 150 cubic meters of balsa wood. That's several tons of balsa wood. This requires cutting down balsa trees that cover an area of about 3 soccer fields. The balsa trees needed for this grow in plantations, but with the growing demand for balsa wood, the plantations cannot meet the demand resulting in the (illegal) cutting of trees in the Amazon.

Birds, bats and insects

Rotating wind turbines are a major hazard to birds, bats and insects. The risk varies by species. Collisions with wind turbines are already the leading cause of death of bats. With the initially small numbers of wind turbines, this was not yet a major problem for the bat population because the number of victims per wind turbine is relatively small. However, with the sharp growth in the number of wind turbines and the size of the area covered by the rotor blades, the numbers of casualties are no longer negligible.

In the case of the historic windmill, by the way, this did not play any role. With a diameter of at most 25 meters, the blades were small and thus covered only a small frontal area (the area of the circle covered by the blades). In addition, the blade area was large: an average blade had a width of 2.25 meters and a length of about 10 meters. As a result, the space between the 4 blades was very small and hardly any passage was possible for birds; for birds they were visible. In addition, the blades of old windmills turned at a much lower tip speed than modern wind turbines. A large historic windmill with a blade diameter of 25 meters rotated at approximately 20 revolutions per minute. The tip of the blade traveled 78.5 meters per revolution - $(2 \times \pi \times r) = (2 \times \pi \times 12.5) = 78.5$. At 20 revolutions per minute, the tip of the blade then traveled $20 \times 78.5 = 1570$ meters. This means that a tip speed of 94 km/hour could be achieved - 60 minutes x 1570 meters. As stated earlier in Chapter 2, modern wind turbines achieve a tip speed of up to about 270 km/hour.

Effects on birds

Proponents of wind turbines often argue that the contribution of wind turbines to bird mortality is insignificant and that many more birds die from other causes, such as domestic cats. This is correct, but in doing so, cats in generally kill small, common, and rapidly reproducing species, such as sparrows, blackbirds, tits, and so on. Moreover, it is often the weakened specimens from the population that a cat manages to capture, and this only applies to land-based wind turbines. Mortality of seabirds is enormous and is increasing as more offshore wind farms are built. But it is not just about bird mortality. The negative effects of modern wind turbines on birds can be divided into 3 categories, namely:

- direct mortality from contact with rotor blades,

- habitat loss - loss of habitat – and,

- barrier effect.

Direct mortality refers to birds flying to their death against the rotor blades or pylon of the wind turbine. This occurs particularly at night and in bad weather. Birds can also die or be (fatally) injured by the air vortices caused by rotating rotor blades.

Habitat loss occurs because many birds avoid wind farms and their surroundings. Those areas thus become unsuitable as feeding, resting, or nesting areas, thus causing habitat loss for birds. Habitat loss is automatically accompanied by an imbalance in the local ecosystem. After all, birds are prey for certain predators, they contribute to eating insects and spreading seeds.

Barrier effect means that wind farms create barriers for birds. Migratory birds and birds on their way to and from feeding, breeding or resting areas often fly around wind turbines. This costs the birds time and energy, forcing them to eat extra while leaving less foraging time. Another effect of this is lower breeding success, since young birds are left alone longer and must wait longer for food.

More than 400 bird species are in the Netherlands throughout the year. By no means all species are equally at risk of `direct mortality, habitat loss and/or barrier effect by wind turbines. Aspects that play a role here include body weight and flight altitude but also the time of year - migratory bird, breeding bird, winter visitor. According to the North Sea Foundation, some 80 million birds fly over the North Sea every year. Above land, there are even hundreds of millions. A number of bird species have been identified as most vulnerable to direct mortality and habitat loss on land and at sea.[6]

Vulnerable bird species on land
The most vulnerable species to direct mortality from collisions with land-based wind turbines are raptors, migratory birds, and owls. Large numbers of migratory birds fly between their breeding and wintering grounds in the spring and fall. During migration, they are at significant and increasing risk of colliding with wind turbines in or near their established migration routes, especially at night and in adverse weather conditions such as headwinds, fog, and rain, when they fly lower. Other sensitive bird species include larks, storks, lapwings and plovers, cranes, and gulls. Meadow birds and other species that live on open land are the most sensitive to habitat loss due to wind turbine construction. This is because they try to avoid high-rise structures in the open landscape where they nest.

Vulnerable bird species at sea
Gulls such as kittiwake, great skua, great black-backed gull, little black-backed gull and herring gull are known to be very sensitive to collisions with offshore wind turbines. Real seabirds such as gannets, guillemots, auk and all types of divers will avoid wind farms.[7]

At sea, species such as the shelduck, sanderling, knot, little swan, brent goose, starling, curlew, and black tern are among the most vulnerable among migratory birds.

Adverse effects on bird populations
Additional bird mortality from collisions with wind turbines can lead to a decline in the bird population. Barrier effects also affect this. Combined with habitat loss, this leads to imbalance in the local ecosystem.Under the Nature Conservation Act, the impact of wind farms must remain within the ecological preconditions of protected species. This means that, before a permit for new wind farms is given, a legal assessment is made whether the numbers of protected species are not reduced too drastically by those wind farms. After all, that is not allowed.

There are two commonly used methods for determining whether wind farms are responsible for what is known as "acceptable bird mortality". Under the Extra Mortality Method (EMM), a small increased mortality on top of natural mortality is considered acceptable. The effect of, say, 1-5% more mortality, would then be negligible. In addition, Potential Biological Removal (PBR) is considered. This is a term from the hunting and fishing world that calculates the part of a population that can be removed without major consequences. Both methods are often used in the Netherlands and internationally as a basis for licensing.

Fig. 6.2: Flocks of birds near wind turbines.

Based on both of these methods, researchers from Wageningen University looked at how "acceptable mortality" according to standards affects populations of the starling, godwit, marsh harrier, spoonbill, stork, common tern, and sea eagle. The results show that population size can be highly sensitive to a small increase in mortality (ESM). Instead of a negligible effect, the researchers found that 1% additional mortality resulted in a 2 to 24% decrease in the number of birds of the various bird species after 10 years. At 5% additional mortality, it resulted in a decrease in populations after 10 years of 9 to as much as 77%, depending on the species. Starlings are particularly sensitive to additional mortality. Short-lived species such as the starling already have naturally high mortality rates and are therefore very sensitive to a small percentage increase in mortality.

The results thus show that the impact of mortality from wind turbines on bird populations can be large, regardless of whether "one" considers the additional mortality acceptable on legal grounds. Nature itself, of course, does not care about our models. So, the effects do not always turn out to be negligible, as is often assumed. This is especially true for species that are already having a hard time in the Netherlands, such as the marsh harrier, the common tern and the godwit. Besides the fact that the methods used to calculate the impact of wind turbines on bird populations give incorrect results, it is important that the cumulative mortality in the area where a population occurs is included in the mortality estimate. Now, mortality is often estimated only in relation to an individual wind farm. However, bird populations increasingly encounter wind turbines in the landscape.[8][9]

It is important to realize that the impact assessments carried out in the licensing of wind turbines are largely only theoretical estimates. Very much about the actual numbers of victims and the actual effects at bird population level is still unknown, and this is especially true for the cumulative (total) effects of all existing and planned wind farms.

Figures on the effects on bird populations threatened by large numbers of wind turbines, such as the red kite in Germany, have been known for some time. The red kite is one of the most strictly protected bird species in Europe. As many as half of the world's red kite population lives in Germany, and Rheinland-Pfalz is in the core area of their distribution. In a 2014 study conducted by the bird protection organization in the Federal State of Brandenburg, a comparison was made for the first time between the calculated and actual numbers of red kites dying from wind turbine rotor blades.[10] Over several months, the number of casualties was counted. In Brandenburg alone, more than 300 red kites were found to be killed annually by wind turbines in wind farms. The figures from Brandenburg also apply to other regions where red kites are common, according to the researchers.

Fig. 6.3: Instead of poplars there are wind turbines on the dyke...

On average, 10 wind turbines were responsible for the death of one red kite annually. So with 1400 wind turbines, which was the number installed in Rheinland-Pfalz in 2014, that would result in 140 dead red kites per year. The Rheinland-Pfalz government assumed much lower numbers in its casualty statistics. Since the introduction of those statistics, only seven red kites were officially recorded as victims of wind turbines there. So the statistics did turn out to be very different from practice, which drew criticism. Rheinland-Pfalz allegedly only relied on some accidental findings and spot checks, thus closing its eyes to reality. There are fewer wind turbines in Rheinland-Pfalz than in the state of Brandenburg, but only one red kite death due to a rotor blade had been recorded there, which was used as the basis for the "official calculations".

When the authorities do not do their job properly, as in this case regarding the red kite, this has far-reaching consequences for (protected) bird species. There seems to be a lack of political will to conduct systematic research on bird collision victims. Is one afraid of the outcome? Also in the Netherlands, the effects of wind turbine placement are determined mostly theoretically.[11] This means that estimates of effects on bird populations are made without measuring these effects. This will eventually have dramatic consequences for certain bird species.

Effects on bats

Bats, like any living thing, have an important function in the ecosystem. Bats are natural insect catchers. They are also very important for pollinating flowers and dispersing seeds. In fact, many tropical plants depend entirely on bats for reproduction. Worldwide, there are about 1.500 different species of bats. All over the world, however, bat species are threatened, by loss or fragmentation of habitat, decline in food supply, destruction of habitats and hunting for processing into traditional "medicines." In fact, collisions with wind turbines have now become one of the leading causes of bat mortality throughout North America and Europe. There is, therefore, a growing concern for bat conservation around the world. The 2012 estimate of annual bat fatalities from wind turbines in the United States ranged from 600.000-888.000 bats.

At that time, wind power capacity there was 51.630 megawatts (MW), representing 12-17 fatalities per year per MW of installed capacity. By 2019, estimates were already above 3 million dead bats per year, based on numbers of victims found by search dogs in and around wind turbines in wind farms. Searching for victims by search dogs instead of humans appears to give a much better picture of the actual numbers of victims. Research in Europe shows that the numbers of bat casualties are comparable.[12][13][14]

Despite conservation concerns for many bat species, factors causing mortality in bats had not been studied since 1970. That changed in 2016 with a study by O'Shea et al.[15] That study involved mapping cause of death among 152 species of bats across all continents from the year 1790 onwards. Figure 6.4 summarizes the cause of death of the 1180 dead bats reported. What particularly emerged from the study is the strikingly high numbers of bats killed by wind turbines in North America and Europe starting in the year 2000. Wind turbines emerged in the study as the number one cause of death.

There are no other well-documented threats to populations of migrating bats that cause mortality of a similar magnitude. It does appear that migrating bats are somehow attracted to the rotor blades of wind turbines.[16]

Bats are primarily active between sunset and sunrise, when temperatures are above 11.5°C and wind speeds are below 5 m/s. Consequently, most bat deaths occur in late summer - a period with relatively low winds and high temperatures. In principle, the available data make it possible to significantly reduce the number of collisions by turning off wind turbines in late summer when winds are not so strong anyway. Doing so could achieve as much as a 50% to 75% reduction in bat incidents.

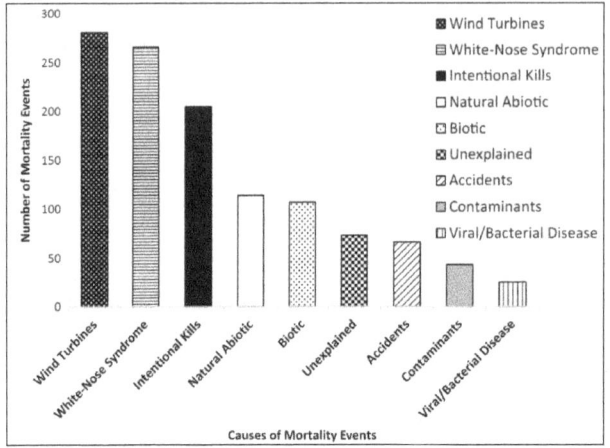

Fig. 6.4: Summary of cause of death of 1180 reported dead bats among 152 species worldwide, by O'shea et al.

To do this requires cooperation from the energy companies. This is because it means an intervention in the control of the wind turbines and a reduced yield. However, that required cooperation turns out to be very small. For 75% of Germany's onshore wind turbines no measures appear to have been taken. Moreover, new counts show that for wind turbines that are not switched off, the number of victims is much higher than previously estimated: an average of 70 bats die every 2 months per wind turbine. There are currently about 30.000 wind turbines in Germany, so the number of victims runs into the millions. No numbers are known for the Netherlands, but there is no reason to believe that the figures here would be more favorable. In 2030, if the energy transition continues, the installed capacity will be three times as large as it is now, so the number of victims will continue to increase.[17][18] This will continue until the number of annual casualties becomes smaller and smaller, as bat populations will automatically become smaller and smaller.

Measures for populations.

To reduce bird and bat casualties, other measures can also be taken. A first option is to install a camera detection system. As soon as it detects a bird or bat, the wind turbine shuts down. It is estimated that the cost of such a system can be as much as 100.000 euros over the lifetime of the wind turbine. In addition, losses occur because there will be more downtime of the wind turbine. For these reasons, wind farm operators are not exactly eager to equip their wind turbines with these detection systems.

Painting one of the three rotor blades of a wind turbine black could also reduce bird collisions with the rotor blades. The underlying idea is that one black rotor blade between two white ones makes the wind turbine more recognizable to birds as a rotating object. A study is currently underway at Eemshaven to further investigate the effect. Based on the results of that initial study, the Human Environment and

Transport Inspectorate wants to consider a broader application by, among other things, conducting a similar test at offshore wind farms. If the results are positive, there are still a number of complications for implementation. First, there are UN and EU laws and regulations that stipulate that the color of wind turbines, for both the pylon and the rotor blades, must be white. This may only be deviated from if it is demonstrated that this does not lead to more unsafe situations for air traffic. In addition, it is still unclear whether there are technical objections to color differences. There are indications that color differences shorten the lifetime of the turbines. The main reason is that dark surfaces heat up faster and more strongly, causing them to expand more than white surfaces. This can lead to stresses in the structure, decreasing service life. The additional costs, if any, that will result from this are currently unknown, which may be a stumbling block for wind turbine manufacturers. The earliest the results of ongoing research will be known is 2024, so it will be some time before such a measure might be implemented. In the meantime, wind turbines continue to spin, their numbers increase and millions of bird and bat deaths occur.[19]

Effects on insects

That birds and bats fall victim to wind turbines in large numbers is obvious. There have also been several reports in recent years that insects are also doing badly. It is known that the total number of flying insects in northern Germany has declined by more than 75 percent in 27 years.[21] This is also reflected in the number of insects that end up on car windshields today. That number is many times smaller than it was 10 or 20 years ago.

It is not exactly known what causes this decline. However, research by Dr. Franz Trieb of the "Institute of Engineering Thermodynamics" has made it clear that wind turbines on land, at least, contribute greatly to insect mortality.[22] Migrating, flying insects seek out high and fast air currents in large swarms to be transported to distant breeding sites. During this journey, they appear to be hit in large numbers by rotor blades. Moreover, insect precipitation on rotor blades also adversely alters the airflow around the blades, reducing the performance of wind turbines.

A rough but still conservative estimate of the impact of wind farms on flying insects in Germany, according to Trieb's research, results in a loss of about 1.2 trillion insects of various species per year. That's 1.200 billion, or 1.200.000.000.000 insects.

Several species of insects migrate, thus limiting the impact of wind farms not only to local insect populations. In fact, some

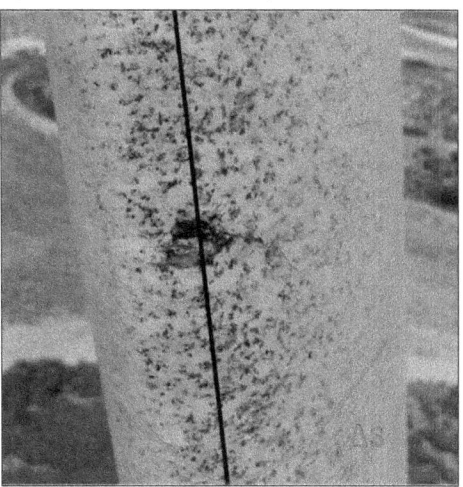

Fig. 6.5: Crushed insects on a rotor blade.[20]

species of insects migrate many hundreds to thousands of miles, and the likelihood of encountering a wind farm along the way is increasing. An example is the thistle butterfly that migrates north from Africa every year. Usually, the first butterflies arrive in the Netherlands in May and June. Under favorable weather conditions and depending on the route, it probably takes them one to two weeks to fly from Africa to the Netherlands.

Up to here, the effects of wind turbines on airborne life have been explained for the most part with concrete examples. The large-scale, planned construction of wind turbines at sea, in addition to its effect on bird populations living there, also has consequences for marine life. These consequences are caused not only by the wind turbines themselves, but, as we saw, also by the construction of the necessary infrastructure. Before we look at this in more detail, the plans for the construction of large-scale wind farms in the North Sea will be explained.

The North Sea: from nature to industrial wind turbine field

That the North Sea is intended territory for building large-scale offshore wind farms is now no secret. In 2016, through a joint political declaration, the North Seas Energy Cooperation (NSEC) was launched with the aim of accelerating the construction of wind farms in the North Sea in a cost-efficient manner. On Dec. 2, 2021, a revised version of that political declaration was signed at a ministerial meeting by NSEC members and the European Union. This revised version responds to the European Union's sharpened green agenda since the first declaration signed in 2016. NSEC members are Belgium, France, Denmark, Germany, Ireland, Luxembourg, the Netherlands, Norway, Sweden, and the European Commission.[23]

The North Sea has a surface area of 750.000 km2. The North Sea bottom consists mainly of sand, but in some parts (especially outside the Dutch part) there are gravel banks, the rock surface comes to the surface or spectacular underwater canyons have formed. The average depth of the North Sea is 94 meters.

Plans for building wind farms in the North Sea are shown in Figure 6.6.[24] Eventually, as much as 25% of the total area of the North Sea will be filled with wind farms.[25] This corresponds to an area of 187.500 km2, an area that the Netherlands can fit into 18 times in terms of surface area.

At first it seems logical to place wind turbines at sea, since the wind there blows more often, harder, and more consistently. However, the North Sea harbors special marine life that must be considered. The number of porpoises in the North Sea was estimated at 350.000 animals in 2020. It is also home to soft corals, seahorses and basking sharks, the largest animal in the North Sea at 12 meters long. [26]

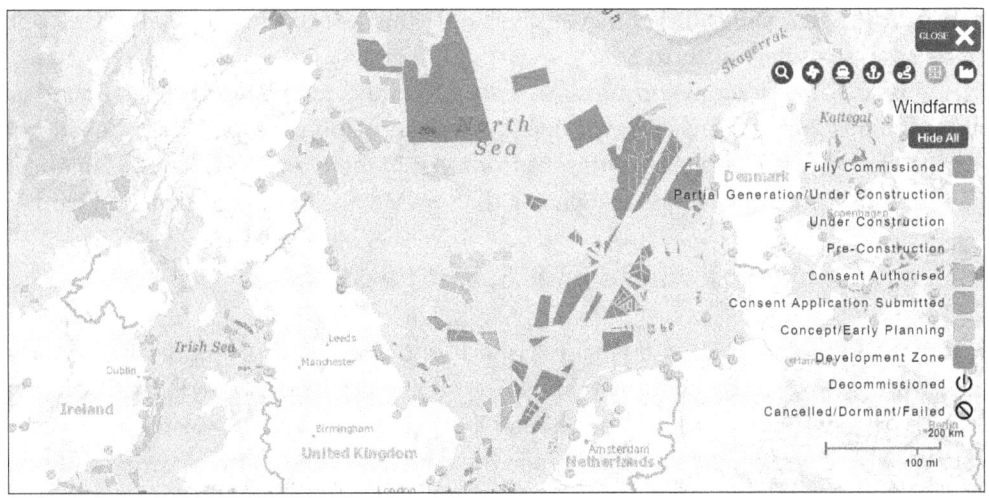

Fig. 6.6: Overview of existing, under construction, planned and wind farms to be developed in the North Sea.

On the bottom of the North Sea, in addition to flatfish, live numerous other bottom-dwelling animals called benthos. The benthos includes starfish, worms, shellfish, snails, and crustaceans. Within the wind at sea ecological program (WOZEP), research has been conducted on the development of the benthic community in the wind farm itself.[27] For example, in the *Princes Amalia* wind farm, benthic developments on the soft substrate, the sandy bottom, have been investigated since 2003. Seabed inspections were conducted in 2003, 2012, 2013 and 2017. This involved comparisons between locations within the wind farm and reference locations outside it. The results of this benthic survey were published in 2018.[28] One of the conclusions of the study is that there is a temporary effect of a wind farm on benthic biodiversity. Biodiversity does not only decrease in the first few years after the wind farm is built. The study shows that a very sharp decline in soil life and biodiversity can also be observed between the 2013 and 2017 measurements. This sharp decline cannot be explained and thus it is uncertain if, and to what extent, wind farms affect benthos biodiversity in the long term. In short, after 14 years of research, it is not yet possible to conclude what the long-term effects of a wind farm on benthic life in the North Sea are.

Despite the results of this study, the construction and operation of wind farms continues. In doing so, the policy does state that nature will be taken into account by, for example, creating oyster beds. However, there is no evidence that life on the seabed will not be drastically altered by this form of human intervention in a natural habitat.

In addition to the impact of wind farms on seabed life, nature is also greatly affected by the pile driving for construction, which involves intense underwater noise. As discussed in Chapter 2, the pile driving exposes a large area of the sea to constant noise. This causes porpoises and seals to become disoriented. This is because they communicate with sound waves, and these become disturbed. Despite mandatory noise-reducing measures during pile driving, some of which are implemented by the construction companies, it is not yet clear how this affects the populations of porpoises and seals in the North Sea.

Plans to fill seas with wind turbines are not limited to the North Sea. Countless plans for this are in the works worldwide, including along the U.S. East Coast. The marine life there is completely different from that in the North Sea. On the American East Coast, it is mainly humpback whales that are victims of the construction work.

Impact on humpback whales on U.S. East Coast

It is often in the news: "large whale washed up on beach at..." Impressive reports, usually accompanied by pictures that capture the imagination. Images that also give us a good impression of what huge animals live in our seas, animals we normally never see. We always read that "scientists are in the dark" as to the cause of the stranding... Could wind farms also be one of the causes?

According to recent reports from the United States National Oceanic and Atmospheric Administration (NOAA), there has been an alarming increase in the number of dead humpback whales washed ashore along the East Coast of the United States for several years. NOAA is currently investigating the deaths of as many as 178 dead whales.[29] The data of "unusual mortality" are astonishing. In fact, the humpback mortality rate roughly tripled from 2016 and remained high thereafter, with the exception of 2021.

Use of Multibeam sonar
Their stranding began mysteriously in 2016, just before the offshore wind turbine industry along the U.S. East Coast took off. At about the same time, seabed mapping began for the construction of wind farms near New Jersey, New York, Delaware and Massachussets. This was done under a concession, which included an exception to the law of marine mammal protection. This exception allowed the depth of the seafloor to be mapped with sonar technology. In this process, research vessels with multibeam sonars emit sound in a fan-shaped pattern. The multibeam sonar emits several pulses of sound at different angles at once.
The pulses are transmitted several times per second in frequencies of between 200-700 kHz. The sonar reflections from the seafloor are then collected. Research has shown that lower frequencies - between 90-130 kHz - are also emitted by the multibeam sonars. These frequencies emitted by this technology are known to be audible to various whale species up to hundreds of meters away.[30] Although the sonar sound is soft, these tones can be heard by whales and dolphins and thus influence the animals' behavior. This can cause whales to die in several ways. When whales flee from the sonar sound, it can lead to collisions with ships or becoming entangled in fishing gear, the two leading unnatural causes of death for whales. In addition, whales may go into a stunned state due to the sound, increasing the likelihood of later colliding with a vessel. Finally, direct bleeding injuries can occur, such as damaging the whales' auditory bone, possibly leading to death by infection.

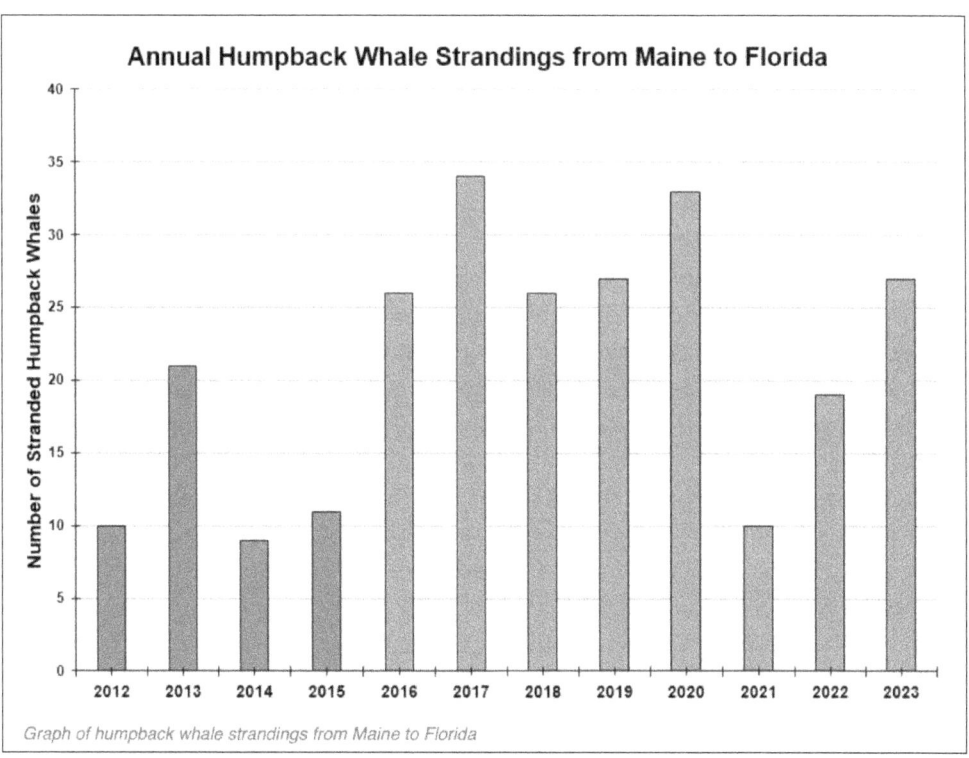

Fig. 6.7: Number of stranded humpback whales off the US East Coast by year; 2023 data are unfortunately only up to summer.

There may be a considerable time between the whale's harmful exposure to the sonar sounds and its death, making it difficult to establish a direct causal relationship. Indeed, whales can travel distances of more than 200 kilometers per day. Thus, a sonar explosion, or location-characterization in one spot, could easily lead to whale deaths hundreds of kilometers away.

Sound made during pile driving also plays an important role in the disorientation of whales.[31] Sound travels through water at a speed of over 1.500 meters per second (5.400 km/h) and carries very far. In water, sound can be heard up to about 100 kilometers away. The noise standard for underwater pile driving is 168 dB at a 750 meter distance from the pile.[32] In comparison, for humans, hearing damage occurs as of 120 dB.

Disturbances caused by cabling on the seabed

Across the bottom of oceans and seas now lie countless data and power cables. In fact, the North Sea is one of the most cabled seas in the world. Most of the cables are on Dutch territory. In fact, cables go from the Netherlands to several countries; The United Kingdom, Belgium, Germany, Denmark, and Norway.[33] The North Sea is tiny compared to the Atlantic Ocean, yet there are over 6.000 kilometers of cables in the Dutch section alone. Also, in the Belgian part is over 1.100 kilometers of cables for electricity and telecom. That does not include gas pipelines. If the plans for all the new wind farms in the North Sea go ahead, the number of kilometers of cabling for electricity will increase significantly.

In addition to the ground disturbance that occurs when the cables are pulled - a trench must be pulled that is sealed when the cable is laid - there are other influences on marine life on the bottom. These are the heat coming off the cables and the electromagnetic field around the cables.[34]

The pulling of the cables results in underwater noise. The benthos, fish, migratory fish, seals, porpoises, and other dolphins may be affected by this underwater noise. The exact impact on these animals is not known. What is known is that underwater noise influences the behavior of seals up to 5 km away. Also, in shallow parts of the sea, foraging birds at that location will be disturbed and their food supply will be affected.

Once the wind farm produces electricity, the power cable will be operational. Because of the current flowing through it, heat will be produced by the cable. Therefore, the temperature in the vicinity of the buried cable will be higher than the local water temperature. At a cable depth of 1.5 meters, the temperature increase at 10 cm below the bottom surface can be as much as over 1.5°C as a result.[34] This affects shellfish and bottom fish. However, it is argued that this temperature increase is negligible compared to the natural temperature variation and that is the reason no further research is being done on it.

Possibly more importantly, many marine animals are very sensitive to electromagnetic fields around cables. Sharks, for example, use electromagnetic waves to detect their prey. Eels, turtles and shellfish also depend on them. They use electromagnetic waves to avoid predators, locate food grounds and migrate thousands of kilometers each year. Research into the effects of electromagnetic radiation is costly, complicated and also difficult to conduct. Will that be why very limited research has been conducted on the effects of electromagnetic radiation on marine life? Aside from a few studies, there have been mostly anecdotal observations to date. For example, from fishermen who report catching flatfish on the east side of a cable, but not on the west side.[35] These are indications that something is going on underwater around power lines.

The studies and publications on the effect of electromagnetic radiation that do exist show that harmful effects do indeed occur on the seafloor. For example, a new study by scientists at Heriot-Watt University shows that lobster larvae are three times more likely to have growth deformities, with the most common abnormality being crooked tail parts, in addition to impaired eye development.[36] This makes it more difficult for the lobsters, whose average size is reduced anyway due to radiation, to swim and also makes foraging for food more difficult. Thus, the results of this study show that, in general, harmful effects due to electromagnetic radiation occur in animals. Thus, more research is needed to identify the effects of electromagnetic radiation from cabling on marine life.

To minimize the harmful effects of cabling on the seabed, wind turbine companies should at least choose a cable technology with the least electromagnetic radiation. For their construction, companies should additionally consider the life cycles of species in the area. Some animals hibernate, others migrate. Mating time is also a vulnerable period for many species. For benthic animals, it is also important that the cables be laid deep enough into the seabed, so as to minimize exposure of the benthic animals to increased temperature and electromagnetic radiation from the cables.

Weather and climate influence by wind turbine

Wind turbines take energy from the moving air and convert it into electricity usable by us. There are now 200.000 wind turbines around the world. Extracting energy from the air obviously affects the air, so what exactly happens to it? An important question is whether the wind turbines themselves affect the weather and climate? And if so, is that positive or does it have adverse effects?

Scientists have also wondered about this, and in the meantime, there are several publications showing that wind turbines do indeed have significant impacts on both weather and climate. The difference between weather and climate is explained in Chapter 4. First, it is explained how wind turbines can affect the weather.

Influence on weather
A recent KNMI publication dated Nov. 29, 2022, shows that wind turbines do indeed affect the weather.[3] Three effects occur: air temperature changes, humidity changes and wind changes. This weather influence is caused by the rotor blades. Rotating rotor blades disturb the atmosphere. Life on Earth thrives on natural, undisturbed weather systems. For a 5 MW wind turbine, with a pylon height of 130 meters and a rotor diameter of 130 meters, the rotor blades cover - mix - the air layers between an altitude of 65 and 195 meter. Locally this may still have a limited influence, for wind farms with hundreds of wind turbines this is not true.

The temperature of the air decreases with increasing altitude. Therefore, on the mountain it is always colder than in the valley. In dry air, the decrease in temperature is about 1 degree per 100 meters, in moist air it is about 0.6 degrees. Rotor blades cause layers of air to mix with each other. They do this by producing vortices that cause layers of air of different heights to mix with each other. These can be various types of air: dry, wet, hot, and cold. This can cause clouds to dissolve or form, for example. Depending on different weather conditions, the effect is noticeable at a great distance from the wind farm. This is called the wake effect. Figure 6.9 shows an example of the formation of clouds by offshore wind turbines.

The wake effect is the effect a wind farm has on the area in the wind shadow (downstream) of the wind farm. This effect is greatest when the atmosphere is stable, that is, when the sea or earth's surface is colder than the air above it. Over the sea, this happens mostly in spring and early summer. Because colder air is heavier than warm air, there will naturally be less vertical mixing in a stable atmosphere than in an

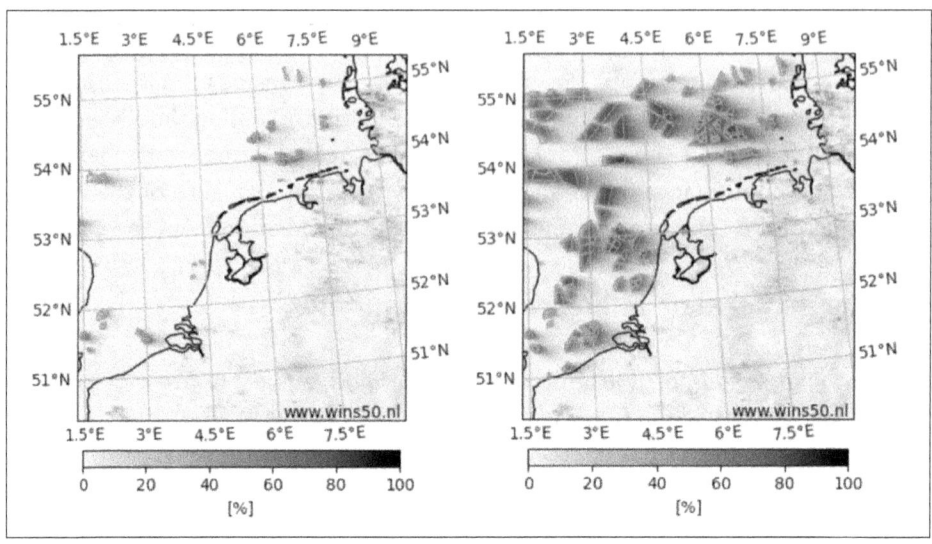

Fig. 6.8: The effect of wind turbines on wind at 100-meter altitude. Wind farms in 2020 (left) and a hypothetical wind farm scenario for 2050 (right) with 2020 weather. Proportion of time (in %) for which the difference in wind speed at 100 m between HARMONIE-AROME with and without wind farms for west wind is larger than 1 m/s.[38] This is a model-based calculation.
Figure 6.9 (below) shows that these are real effects.

unstable atmosphere, where the warm and therefore lighter air is at the bottom and wants to rise. Less mixing with the "undisturbed" layers of air above the wind farm means that wake effects are less likely to be nullified and thus are still present at greater distances from the wind farm.

The effects on temperature and humidity are also greatest in stable situations. Above the sea, the air in the lower layer of the atmosphere in stable weather is not only colder, but also more humid. Wind turbines transport that colder, moister air to layers of air above the turbines' shaft height. For a typical 9 MW offshore wind turbine, that's a height of at least 110 meters. That can mean weather changes in the vicinity of wind turbines at stable conditions, due to fog or cloud formation.

Fig. 6.9: Creation of fog by present offshore wind farm.

In addition, wind farms cause wind to slow down upstream of the wind farm. This is because wind farms create an obstacle. Like apartment buildings, the wind will find a way around and over them.

Because it is planned to have more and more wind farms, both onshore and offshore, wind farms will be in each other's wind shadow much more often in 2050. Figure 6.8, where the situation is sketched for westerly winds, shows in color what part of the time the wind at 100 meters height decreases by more than 1 m/s due to the presence of wind turbines. In stable situations, a decrease in wind speed is sometimes still visible 50-150 km from the wind farm - wind shadow. Especially the coastal regions of the Netherlands and the areas along the IJsselmeer will experience a decrease in wind speed at 100 meters height due to the wind turbines for a large part of the time. This will affect the weather.

Impact on climate
So that there are effects on the weather is clear. But can there also be effects on climate?

To understand this, consider walking on a sandy beach when the sun is burning. On the dry parts of the beach, it feels very hot to the feet, but that changes as soon as the feet arrive on the wetter sand near the water. There it feels much cooler. The cause of the hot sand is the lack of water in the soil. In fact, soil water causes some of the incoming solar radiation to be used for evapotranspiration - the sum of evaporation of soil moisture and transpiration by plants. And energy used for evapotranspiration cannot warm the surface. In other words, when the soil is moist, only a limited portion of the incoming solar radiation is used to warm the earth's surface - and subsequently the air above it. Thus, when the soil is drier, the soil and also the air above it warms up faster.

But what does that have to do with wind turbines and climate? That becomes clear when the impact of wind turbines on soil temperature and moisture is considered.

Influence on soil temperature and moisture management
An American study from 2012[39] examined the impact of wind turbines on soil temperatures in a wind farm. This was compared to the soil temperature in surrounding areas where there are no wind turbines. The soil temperature in the wind farm was found to have increased by 0.72°C over a 10-year period compared to surrounding areas. The explanation was that rotor blades transport warm air from higher air layers downward at night. Water from the resulting heated soil evaporates and causes the soil to become drier.

A more recent publication from Germany dated May 2023 also shows the link between soil dryness and the presence of wind turbines.[40] Soil moisture is tracked throughout Germany in the 'Dürremonitor des Helmholtz Zentrums für Umweltforschung'. In addition, the 'Bundesamt für Naturschutz' tracks where and how many wind turbines are located throughout Germany. The publication clearly shows that there is a connection between the dryness of the soil and the number of wind turbines. This means that wind turbines on land cause warming. The soil temperature rises, the soil becomes drier and the air above the ground becomes warmer as a result. So wind turbines on land cause the opposite effect than what they are intended for: they cause climate change when they should counteract it.

Acoustic pollution

Nearby residents of wind turbines complain about the noise. This is because rotating blades make noise because of the high speed at which they cleave through the air. As mentioned in Chapter 2, the tip of a rotor blade can reach a speed of up to 270 km/hour. In addition, the Dutch RIVM's 'fact sheet on low-frequency noise' shows that in recent years the Dutch GGD has increasingly heard complaints about low humming tones, more so than the 'normal' noise.[41] This so-called infrasonic sound has such a low frequency that it is inaudible to the human ear. However, a characteristic of infrasonic sound is that it carries much further than "ordinary" sound. It also causes vibrations indoors. True, there are more sources of very low tones in our living environment, such as machinery, pumps, and road and rail traffic, but an important characteristic of wind turbines is that they rotate a large part of the time and thus produce a constant infrasonic sound for long periods of time. These are very low vibrations of air, soil or water that can be very powerful and, like "ordinary" noise, can cause health complaints. These include complaints such as sleep disorders, dizziness, tinnitus, nausea, headaches, loss of concentration, loss of hearing, memory loss, restlessness, but also high blood pressure, heart rate problems, bronchitis, anxiety, brain damage and sometimes depression.[42]

Many thousands of people in the Netherlands experience some degree of noise pollution from wind turbines daily. Dutch research shows that in our country about two percent of the population is severely annoyed by some form of infrasonic noise.[42] The infrasonic noise from rotating wind turbine blades appears to be the most insidious in this regard.

Modern wind turbines produce about 110 dB of infrasonic noise. At a house 1000 meters away, there is still about 35 dB of that. This is because low-frequency infrasonic sound is much less attenuated than higher-frequency sound. Wind turbines in the Netherlands may not produce more than an average of 47 dB 'at the facade' per day and a maximum of 41 dB on average at night. This standard is an annual average, in other words, if a wind turbine produces excessively loud noise for long periods during high winds, but much less when there is no wind, the wind turbine can remain below the standard on average.

To limit the impact on public health in terms of noise from wind turbines, there is actually only one real solution: wind turbines must be located at a sufficient distance from built-up areas. Recently, noise standards have been tightened in Canada, Denmark, and Germany (Beieren). However, a greater distance between people and wind turbines on land is difficult due to the limited space and high population density in the Netherlands. The acceleration of wind turbine construction combined with the failure to tighten noise standards is expected to lead to increasing problems for public health.

> **Infrasound**
>
> Just how damaging infrasonic sound can be was demonstrated when the United States withdrew much of its embassy staff from Cuba in 2017. Indeed, more than 20 diplomats fell ill, due to an infrasonic sound attack.[43] Infrasonic sound is considered a weapon by the US military, and since the early 1990s its negative impact on life species with inner ear structures has been known. Sufficient distance from the source is the only remedy against infrasonic sound.

Various articles and interviews in the media reveal that residents living near wind turbines are so disturbed by the noise that they regularly flee their homes at night to sleep in their cars several miles away.

When the human body is exposed to infrasonic sound for long periods of time, thickening of the pericardium, a membrane surrounding the heart, can occur. As a result, pre-existing heart problems can worsen. People with pre-existing heart problems are also more likely to have a stroke and/or a heart attack.[44]

Jan de Laat, audiologist at Leiden University Medical Center (LUMC), analyzed more than three hundred recent global studies on health aspects of infrasonic sound, among other things. In his research, De Laat found multiple indications of a link between infrasonic sound exposure and heart problems.

Dropshadow

The rotor blades of wind turbines produce dropshadows on a sunny day. The rotating blades cause these shadows to move continuously at a certain frequency. This has the effect of a flashing light. The dropshadow is longest at sunrise and sunset in winter.

People who live in the dropshadow of a wind turbine report experiencing great annoyance. Shadow causes annoyance and concentration problems because it is constantly distracting. If the dropshadow falls on the bedroom window, sleep problems can occur. The overall consequence is increased stress.

Whether dropshadow occurs at a residence depends on many factors, such as the season, time of day, location in relation to the wind turbine, wind direction and, of course, whether the sun is shining. At a low position of the sun, the dropshadow of a wind turbine with a tip height of 232 meters reaches 4 km far. In winter, the dropshadow from the same wind turbine reaches 900 meters in the middle of the day. This means that a lot of people will potentially be affected.

Dropshadow may not move indefinitely over facades of "sensitive objects". Sensitive objects are homes, educational buildings, hospitals, nursing homes, care homes, psychiatric institutions, day care centers, caravan sites and moorings for houseboats. Businesses do not fall into the "sensitive objects" category. The so-called "Environmental Management Activities Decree" sets the standard in the

Netherlands that a maximum dropshadow duration of 20 minutes per day for an average of 17 days per year is acceptable.

It follows from the "Environmental Management Regulations" that wind turbines must have an automatic standstill device in certain situations. This applies when dropshadow occurs at the location of sensitive objects (usually houses) to the extent that the distance between the wind turbine and the houses or other sensitive objects is less than 12 times the rotor diameter and on average more than 17 days per year for more than 20 minutes per day dropshadow can occur. With a rotor diameter of 120 meters (the rotor blade is then 60 meters), the distance between the wind turbine and the residence in that case must be less than 12 x 120 meters, or 1440 meters. The standstill device ensures that at certain times, when the sun shines, the wind turbine is stopped. As a result, varying levels of cast shadow do not occur at that time. A computer system keeps track of all the data and automatically triggers shutdown. A sensor on the wind turbine measures light incidence. The turbine is then in the so-called idle mode. There is then always still a very slow movement to prevent wear on bearings, which occurs at a complete standstill.

After the commissioning of a wind turbine, one of the things that must be adjusted is the shutdown facility. This requires a great deal of coordination for each turbine and each home. This adjustment can take several months, during which time it can cause frustration and complaints from local residents.

When the first homes around a wind turbine are at a distance just slightly greater than 12 times the rotor diameter, there is no need to consider cast shadow. Therefore, people who live there face a lot of dropshadow.[45]

Decline in value of homes

Meanwhile, it has become clear that people do not like to live near wind turbines. And besides the nuisance of noise and dropshadow, there is also such a thing as horizon pollution.

Wind turbines affect the value of surrounding homes.[46] Quantitative data on the decline in the value of homes near wind turbines were examined by research institute TNO on behalf of the Ministry of Economic Affairs and Climate Change. It looked at homes at between 1.5-2.5 kilometers from a wind turbine. Houses located there are worth an average of 3.8% less compared to houses in places where there are no wind turbines. Over the period 2020-2030, this means a reduction in value of 9.295 euros per house on average, based on the value of the house in 2020. In total, this means that 15.5 billion euros in value is lost in the Netherlands.

The increase in the decrease in the value of homes is mainly caused by the increase in the height of wind turbines and their increased numbers. Thus, more and more homes are affected by wind turbines. The number of homes located between 1.5-2.5 kilometers from wind turbines will increase from 900.000 in 2020 to about 1.600.000 in 2030 if plans to build additional wind farms are realized. The proportion of homes affected by this drop in value will therefore rise from 12% to 22%.[47]

As for the number of houses and the decrease in value of houses within 1.5 kilometers of wind turbines, no exact numbers can be found.

So far, the direct effects of wind turbine operation on people and nature have been discussed. The production, construction and operation of wind turbines also involve the use of a variety of harmful substances. The most important ones are briefly discussed below.

Fig. 6.10: Horizon pollution from wind turbines.

SF6 for electrical insulations

The first of the substances leading to harmful effects is sulfur hexafluoride (SF6). While the gas is harmless to humans and animals, if there are any so-called greenhouse gases at all, according to the IPCC, SF6 is the strongest greenhouse gas known, as much as 23.900 times stronger than CO_2.[48] That governments allow the use of SF6 is thus highly inconsistent in the context of the intended reduction of CO_2 emissions.

The IPCC states that it takes 3.200 years for SF6 to break down in the atmosphere after which it only loses its greenhouse effect. Remarkably, SF6 does not appear in the climate agreement, although it was mentioned in Kyoto in 1992 as an extremely important greenhouse gas to be avoided. In the 1990s, fluorine gas was still used in tennis balls, the soles of athletic shoes and in double glazing. However, this is no longer allowed after a European ban in 2014.

SF6 has been used since the 1960s to insulate switching stations in the power grid, up to transformer boxes in residential areas. It is mainly used in medium- and high-voltage substations. It is also widely used in wind turbines. For power companies and wind turbine manufacturers, the use of SF6 is a necessary evil. It is an excellent insulation material, and its application reduces the chances of short circuits and arcs between different conductors. In addition, SF6 can extinguish flames.

British research from 2018 has shown that leakage of SF6 occurs at facilities where the gas is incorporated. So this includes wind turbines,[49] where leaks can occur due to mechanical failure, wear and tear of components or during maintenance or decommissioning.

According to Netbeheer Nederland, 770 kilograms of SF6 leaked through all network companies combined in the Netherlands in 2018, the equivalent of some 18 million kilograms of CO_2 in terms of greenhouse effect.[50] Observations from weather stations in Britain, Ireland and Australia show that the amount of SF6 in the atmosphere has increased by tens of percent during recent years. Germany has discovered by measurement that the air over Germany contains much more of this very dangerous gas SF6 than in other countries. Could this have something to do with the huge amount of wind turbines located in Germany? The Dutch KNMI does not take measurements of SF6 concentrations in the atmosphere, nor does the Netherlands Emissions Authority monitor them. Network companies themselves must report SF6 leaks to RIVM, but there are no penalties so involved for leaking SF6. In some countries, network companies are fined for excessive leaks.

In the Netherlands, electricity network operators - the network companies Stedin, Enexis, Liander and especially TenneT - are currently busy expanding the medium- and high-voltage grid. This is because new switching stations are needed to connect additional wind farms and fields full of solar panels. SF6 is still being used for those switching stations (with a few exceptions). As a result, the total use of SF6 at Dutch grid companies has continued to rise year after year, from 133.500 kilograms in 2007 to 212.000 kilograms in 2018, according to reports by Netbeheer Nederland. According to wind turbine manufacturer Vestas, about 7 kilograms are used per wind turbine.[51]

The Dutch network companies and three of the largest international switchgear builders - ABB, Siemens, and General Electric - confirm the use of the greenhouse gas. The switchgear manufacturers do test alternatives, but report that SF6 is often still the only stable and most commercial option. The alternatives being tested are NovecTM 4710 and NovecTM 5110 (from manufacturer 3M) and synthetic air, a mix of oxygen and nitrogen (O_2/N_2).[52]

However, structural solutions for high-voltage switchgear are still a long way off, even though, when asked, all Dutch grid companies indicate that they are open to new solutions to be developed. Network operators are conservative. After all, they have to ensure a reliable grid and therefore take fewer risks with unknown alternatives. Price often plays a decisive role in this. SF6 will therefore continue to be used in the coming years.

Bisphenol-A

A second substance used in wind turbines that is very harmful to the environment is the substance bisphenol-A (BPA for short). As described in Chapter 2, the rotor blades of modern wind turbines are manufactured from fiberglass-reinforced epoxy material. BPA is used as the basis for these plastics. Epoxy contains 30-40% BPA. BPA is a synthetic organic compound prepared by the reaction of phenol and acetone, which explains the letter A (acetone) in BPA. BPA is one of the most synthesized plastics in the world. Over the past 10 years, however, concerns about BPAs have been growing because mass production and large-scale use also releases large amounts of it into the environment.

Fig. 6.11: Typical erosion of a leading edge of a rotor blade made of glass fibre reinforced epoxy.

How does BPA enter the environment
Although BPA is incorporated into the epoxy resin during the manufacturing process of rotor blades, it enters the environment through wear and tear. As mentioned, the typical tip speed of modern wind turbines is between 190 and 290 km/hour. The leading edge of the rotor blades encounters dust, rain, hail and snow. At these high speeds a lot of friction and thus wear occurs. First, the applied coating of the rotor blades wears away. The fine dust created afterwards by wear of the epoxy contains high levels of BPA, see Figure 6.11.

BPA is then released from the dust particles, posing a danger to humans and the environment. When BPA is in air, the half-life, the time that half of the BPA is broken down in the environment, is only a few days. In soil and water, however, BPA does not break down as quickly. In soil, the half-life rises to six months, and when BPA has entered groundwater, the half-life has become as much as a year.[53]

Norwegian researchers published a report in July 2021 estimating the amount of BPA entering the environment through rotor blade wear. The result was a shocking

62 kilograms of BPA per wind turbine per year. If this is extended to the amount of BPA that would be released if plans to build a multitude of wind farms in the North Sea go ahead, we are talking about hundreds of thousands of kilograms of BPA per year in the marine environment.[54] While this alarming amount of BPA is hotly disputed - some came out at as little as 150 grams per year - in reality it is unknown exactly how much BPA enters the environment. The fact is, however, that rotor blade wear is releasing BPA into the environment and should be a serious concern when rolling out onshore and offshore wind farms. In any case, the alarming study conducted by the "Norwegian Turbine Group" has caused several alarm bells to go off and the issue to receive more attention.

Wind turbine rotor blades are currently the largest consumers of epoxy plastics. In 2013 alone, 27% (69.000 tons) of all epoxy resin used worldwide went into rotor blade production. Annual global production of BPA is 6 million tons and a significant increase is expected in the coming years to as much as 8 million tons by 2032. This growing production of BPA is particularly anticipated for the automotive and marine industries.[55]

If BPA enters the environment on a large scale through rotor blade wear and tear, among other things, the increasing number of wind turbines could soon cause a major environmental disaster. This concern emerges in part from the fact that BPA causes hormone disruption in humans. Unborn and young children are especially vulnerable because their hormones are still developing. Back in 2012, the World Health Organization (WHO) warned about the carcinogenic properties of endocrine-disrupting substances and concluded that these substances pose a global threat to public health.[56] So it is no wonder that in April 2023, the European Food Safety Authority (EFSA) proposed a significant reduction in dietary intake of BPA from an acceptable daily intake of 4 micrograms in 2015 to 0.2 nanograms per kilogram of body weight and day.[57] The European Commission has categorized BPAs as a substance of "very high concern" since 2016. However, despite this categorization, the wind turbine industry does not have to account for potential BPA emissions. In addition to its hormone-disrupting effects, BPA also poses serious problems for water. When one gram of bisphenol A enters the water of a dam lake, 10 million liters of water become unusable for human use. So, keeping this substance out of the environment is essential.[58]

The effects of BPAs on marine life have been detailed in the biological literature. For example, according to a 2005 study, BPAs can induce so-called "superfeminization" in freshwater snails, even at extremely low concentrations of 1 millionth of a gram per liter.[59] The above experimental study thus confirms the hormone-disrupting effects at low concentrations.

Aerodynamic problems
But erosion of the leading edge of rotor blades is also aerodynamically problematic. Disturbance of the air around the blades creates more resistance, reducing the turbine's efficiency. Repair is therefore necessary, and in some cases the wear is so severe that rotor blades need to be repaired after only 5 years of use. For example, in

March 2018, Siemens Gamesa had to perform an "emergency" rotor blade repair on no fewer than 140 of the 175 turbines of the 630 MW London Array wind farm due to earlier-than-expected erosion of the rotor blade leading edge. A month earlier, Siemens Gamesa had to repair 87 of 111 turbines at a 400 MW wind farm in Anholt, Denmark. Both cases involved 3.6 MW turbines with 120-meter rotor diameters installed in 2013.[60][61] The fact that these relatively small turbines are already showing advanced erosion on such a scale in less than five years highlights the seriousness of the problem facing the (offshore) wind industry. How much material was released into the environment in these cases is not disclosed. How long these repairs will last also remains to be seen; repairs to composite materials typically do not have the same high quality as that of the original product. Thus, the problem can be expected to only worsen. On the one hand, this is due to the increase in the number of wind turbines at sea, where wear is 40% higher anyway than on land. On the other hand, because of the push for larger rotor blade diameters and therefore higher blade speeds, resulting in more wear. Erosion of rotor blades will become much more frequent in the future, leading to necessary repairs. As a result, wind farms will also have to be taken out of service more often.

As explained in Chapter 3, the Regional Energy Strategy (RES) requires that an Environmental Impact Assessment (EIA) be prepared prior to granting a construction permit for wind turbines. Since it has now been conclusively established that wind turbines also cause chemical pollution with hazardous substances such as BPA, it is essential that this issue be included in the EIA. Until now, administrators have mostly uncritically followed the wind energy lobby, but as the adverse effects become increasingly apparent, ignoring them becomes politically relevant.

PFOS rightly caused much controversy. But looking at the Bisphenol-A dossier, the question is whether wind turbines scattered across the landscape are not going to create an equally large and dangerous cloud of dust. When will policymakers wake up or will PFOS repeat itself?

Other risks around wind turbines

Wind turbines pose certain risks. Examples include ice ejection, pylon breakage and the breakage of a turbine blade or nacelle.

For determining risks in the vicinity of wind turbines, the Dutch government uses the "manual on risk zoning for wind turbines". In 2019, this handbook was split into a risk zoning manual and a risk calculation manual. The manual was created and published by the Dutch RIVM in 2019and provides an overview of laws, regulations and policies regarding the risks of wind turbines to the surrounding area. The manual describes how to determine the risks of, for example, ice ejection, pylon breakage and the breakage of a turbine blade or nacelle.

However, the fact that the risks posed by wind turbines are considered does not mean that situations do not arise that could pose a danger to people who are in the vicinity of wind turbines. However, the probability of this happening is low. Incidents that have occurred in the Netherlands in the past include: the breaking off of a wind turbine in Wieringerwaard in 2000, the breaking off of the rotor blades of a wind turbine in the Waardpolder in 2004, and in 2009 a rotor blade landed on the A6 freeway near Lelystad. More recently, there were two incidents that are detailed.

Fig. 6.12: Damage to a motorist's windscreen caused by ice from a wind turbine blade.

Icing on rotor blades

That toxic particulate matter is not the only thing that comes off rotor blades was demonstrated when, on Dec. 17, 2022, a motorist suffered a scare in a falling ice incident.[62] Indeed, driving along the N992, a large piece of ice suddenly fell on her windshield. A witness driving behind her saw that the ice came from the rotor blades of a wind turbine. There were several large chunks of ice on the road. The woman was lucky that the chunk of ice did not go through her windshield. Waiting for roadside assistance, she saw numerous chunks of ice coming off the wind turbines for two hours. In all, it took a whopping 3 hours before the wind turbines were shut down. The N992 is a busy road with a bike path next to it.

Wind turbine breaks down at wind force 6

On January 4, 2023, one of the wind turbines on the wind farm along the dike between Zeewolde and Almere broke off. At the time there were no people around so the damage was limited to a hole in the road surface. The incident occurred at wind force 6 - a brisk but certainly not abnormal wind. At wind force 10, the turbines are normally shut down only to prevent damage.

Fig. 6.13: Photo of the broken wind turbine along the dyke from the Dutch cities Zeewolde to Almere.

A press release about the cause was issued on May 16, 2023. According to Vattenfall, the owner of the wind farm, the wind turbine incident was caused by a defective component in the system that controls the position of a turbine's blades. The part in question had been replaced as recently as fall 2022.

That the breaking down of wind turbines does not only depend on the age of wind turbines also proves the recent incident in Sweden. Indeed, on July 16, 2022, a brand-new wind turbine broke down completely there. It happened in the Nysäter wind farm, one of the largest wind farms in Europe, where 114 Nordex wind turbines of two different types are installed.

Given plans to build large numbers of wind turbines in the coming decades, it seems only logical that regulations and oversight around wind turbine safety should be tightened. Stricter inspections, maximum lifespan and increased quality requirements for wind turbine manufacturers will be necessary to ensure the safety of people in the future. This will then naturally lead to cost increases in already not insignificant system costs.

There are several examples in the United States of wind farms where poor maintenance has led to incidents. An example of the Biglow Canyon Wind Farm in the United States illustrates what the consequences of poor maintenance can be.

Fig. 6.14: Photographs of the broken rotor blade at Biglow Canyon Wind Farm in the United States.

Fig. 6.15: Oil spread by wind turbines due to leaks at Biglow Canyon Wind Farm.

Visualizing the effects of overdue maintenance

Maintenance of wind turbines is an important aspect. High loads and vibrations, rotating parts and wear and tear of components make regular inspections and maintenance necessary to prevent dangerous incidents. In doing so, the safety of residents and passersby must be ensured.

Biglow Canyon Wind Farm is a wind farm in Sherman County, U.S., in the state of Oregon. It is owned by Portland General Electric of Portland (PGE), which began operating it in 2007. The farm consists of 76 Vestas wind turbines with a combined capacity of 125 MW, later supplemented by 141 Siemens wind turbines. This brings the total capacity of the wind farm to 450 MW.

On Feb. 1, 2022, a rotor blade broke off from one of the Vestas wind turbines. A few days before, one of the residents had found broken bolts at that wind turbine. The incident prompted an in-depth investigation into the maintenance of the machines.

This investigation, conducted by 'The Oregonian/OregonLive' revealed that this apparently isolated incident was part of a whole series of under-maintenance problems and failures of wind turbines and peripheral equipment in this wind farm.[63] It appeared, for example, that shutters, metal disks and blade bolts had also previously fallen off turbines. Owner PGE had never reported these incidents and had allowed at least four wind turbines with broken off blade bolts to continue operating as usual.

In addition, the wind turbines in Biglow Canyon were found to have contaminated the surrounding fields due to leaks of oil and lubricants (see Figure 6.15). There had also been two fires due to ruptured transformers in which 3.000 liters of mineral oil spilled into the surrounding soil.

Figure 6.16 shows that owner PGE's operating and maintenance costs have fallen 40% since 2013, despite aging equipment and inflation in the price of wind turbine components.

In 2020, researchers at the Lawrence Berkeley National Lab conducted a study of wind plant performance in the United States. This showed that the performance of wind plants in the United States declines suddenly after 10 years, much more abruptly than output declines in, say, Europe or Asia. The researchers concluded that this is related to federal production subsidies. In fact, those stop after 10 years. Wind farm owners simply decide to cut back on maintenance after the subsidy ends.

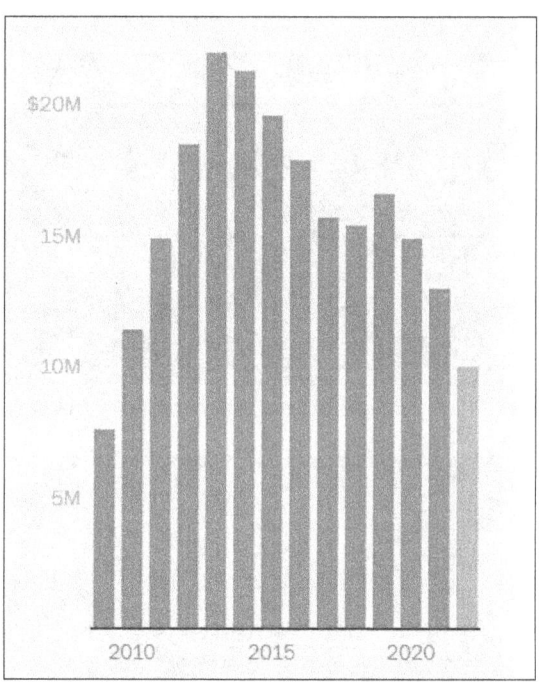

Fig. 6.16: Operating and maintenance costs of Biglow Canyon.[64]

Use and leakage of synthetic oil

Not only due to overdue maintenance does oil from wind turbines leak into nature. After the crash of a brand-new wind turbine in Sweden in 2022, locals were warned about oil leaking out.[65] Many people do not know this, but a wind turbine, depending on its size, requires between 200-800 liters of oil as lubricant for the turbine. An average wind farm has 150 wind turbines. Assuming 300 liters of oil on average per wind turbine, this is a total of 45.000 liters for an average wind farm. This is a synthetic petroleum-based PAO oil and must be replaced once every seven years.[66]

It is estimated that over 7.000 wind turbines are needed to power a city like New York City. That means 300.000 liters of refined oil per year is needed for a city like New York just to replace it. Not to mention what to do with the oil waste.

Currently, it is estimated that there are over 200.000 wind turbines installed worldwide. The same calculation for replacing oil thus comes to an annual refined oil requirement of over 8.6 million liters. To completely phase out fossil fuels, over 2 million more 3 MW turbines need to be installed worldwide, as demonstrated in Simon Michaux's work (see Chapter 2).

The existing wind turbines will have to be replaced in the coming years, as they start to reach the end of their useful life. The same is eventually true of the 2 million wind turbines yet to be built. But what happens to the old wind turbines? Can they be recycled? In other words, what do we do with wind turbine waste?

Wind Turbine Waste

At the end of a wind turbine's useful life, all components must be recycled as much as possible. This follows from governments' recycling targets. The central government wants the Netherlands to have a circular economy by 2050 and has therefore set up the Circular Economy Implementation Program. An economy in which renewable raw materials are used as much as possible, products and raw materials are reused and in which waste does not actually exist. For the metals and concrete used in wind turbines, this is achievable with current technology.

Concrete
Traditionally, old concrete is turned into concrete granules, or small chunks of concrete rubble, by concrete crushers. However, this shredding is done by heavy, energy-intensive machines. 98% of all these granules is currently processed as foundation material, 2% as gravel substitute in new concrete, but more cement is always needed in new concrete for comparable strength and concrete quality.

Metal
Metals are 100% recyclable, and this process can even be repeated several times. The elements that make up the metal can be carefully sorted and reused. Hence,

scrap metal always makes money at the metal trade. Remelting, however, does use a lot of energy.

The problem of rotor blades: fiber-epoxy materials
As far as wind turbine rotor blades are concerned, recycling is an entirely different story. This is because rotor blades (glass fiber and epoxy) do not allow themselves to be recycled with the current state of technology. Since rotor blades are most exposed to wear due to the weather and wind load on the blades, it is not unusual for rotor blades to need to be replaced even during the lifetime of a wind turbine. Annually, this happens to about 2% of the total wind turbines. That means that at the moment, about 40.000 rotor blades are already involved annually.[67] In practice, therefore, the amount of waste from wind turbines on average exceeds the equivalent number of rotor blades.

Most discarded rotor blades end up being incinerated. In Europe alone, as many as 14.000 rotor blades must be disposed of by 2023, said Ramon González-Drigo, a professor at the Polytechnic University of Catalonia in Spain.

Fig. 6.17: Example of rotor blade dumping in the United States.

In the Netherlands and other affluent countries, there are generally adequate regulations in place to prevent the dumping of waste, thus damaging the environment. In large parts of the world, however, this is not the case. Landfills exist in the United States, for example, where thousands of worn-out rotor blades are currently being dumped. The around 20–40 tons, 40-85 meter long, fiberglass epoxy rotor blades with (often) balsa wood are often even dumped illegally. As a result, the bisphenol-A will leak out of the epoxy over time, contaminating groundwater.

In August 2022, a report appeared around an American "blade recycling" company Global Fiberglass Solutions Inc, which was caught illegally storing hundreds of wind turbine blades at three locations in Iowa. All while the company claimed to be recycling the rotor blades. People from the company were charged with dumping more than 1.300 rotor blades in makeshift landfills.

In Oregon, a so-called U.S. rotor blade "recycler" was fined more than $57.000 for dumping hundreds of old rotor blades right next to a natural spring and wetland. The company falsely claimed that the cocktail of 2.741 cubic meters of fiberglass and plastics amounted to "clean fill."[68] That illegal dumping began back in 2019.

A final example comes from the town of Sweetwater, Texas. There, an American company in Nolan County offered a "solution" for disposing of rotor blades that needed to be replaced. The company claimed to store the blades in two facilities and then break them down and resell them to other companies. It later turned out that the company stored all 4.000 rotor blades taken since 2018 but did nothing with them.[69]

Rotor blade recycling, by the way, is reluctantly beginning to take shape. For example, the German company Neocomp in Bremen cuts up rotor blades and then processes them into cement. In recent years, reports have also appeared from wind turbine manufacturers that technological breakthroughs have been made whereby rotor blades may well be recyclable in the future. For example, Vestas published in February 2023 that through new chemical processes it would be possible to separate the epoxy from the glass fibers. In the process, the epoxy could even be completely reused. What this process looks like and whether it involves other environmental implications is not reported.[70]

The inability to recycle fiberglass reinforced epoxy rotor blades remains one of the biggest challenges facing the wind industry currently. It is not inconceivable that positive news about recycling could be spread to ease the increasing pressure on the wind industry to ensure that nothing stands in the way of wind turbine sales. However, whether there will be a technological breakthrough is highly doubtful.

Competing interests

In terms of the adverse environmental impacts described in this book, the wind energy industry has probably seen the storm coming for a long time. According to the University of Twente's 2021 article "Hidden Interests in Wind Turbine Literature," the wind industry is downplaying negative information about the industry through non-independent publications.[71] One of the most frequently cited articles on wind turbines and the possible health effects on humans and animals is Knopper and Ollson's 2011 article titled "Health effects of wind turbines: review of the literature". The authors are purely positive about wind energy and wind turbines, and the negative effects are, in their view, heavily exaggerated. However, the fine print reveals that both authors have worked for the wind turbine industry and are still consultants there. Incidentally, the same is true of the authors of the 2016 book "Alles over Windenergie" by Dutch authors Guido Bakema and Broer Scholtens, who make little or no critical comments about the wind industry. They therefore offer the e-version of their book, published by a marketing agency and stating that it was sponsored by RWE/Essent, or the wind industry, for free on their website.

Speaking of interests, two RIVM publications on wind turbines and their potential harmful effects on human and animal health should be mentioned here. These are the reports "Health effects related to wind turbine sound, GGD Amsterdam & RIVM" from 2017, and "Health effects related to wind turbine sound: an update, RIVM" from 2020. Both reports are frequently cited and used by policy makers in the realization of local wind turbine projects in The Netherlands, including in discussions with concerned citizens. Both RIVM reports make no mention that certain studies are not independent or have been funded by the wind industry. For example, the RIVM 2017 report states on page 16 that "infrasonic noise is not audible," citing Berger and colleagues (2015), the original source. However, this publication is not independent. In fact, the authors of this publication have worked for the wind industry and are now working in wind consulting. Thus, they have an interest in the realization of wind turbines. If you look at the references used by RIVM, it appears that many of them either came from the wind industry itself or were paid by it. For all these articles, the original publication contains a statement of an interest in or funding from the wind industry. However, this is missing from RIVM's reviews.

In this way, the wind industry succeeds in generating a constant stream of positive messages about wind turbines in the public discussion about wind energy. Thereby distracting attention from independent and objective scientific research into the health effects and risks of wind turbines on humans, animals, and the environment. So, administrators and researchers should always look critically at the funding of the original research and what influence industry may have had in scientific publications.

1. www.bnr.nl/nieuws/infrastructuur/10510664/noordzee-krijgt-30-000-windmolens
2. www.interessantetijden.nl/2022/05/31/duits-sprookjesbos-gekapt-voor-windfarm/
3. Documentary Headwind '21 by documentary filmmaker Marijn Poels; www.youtube.com/watch?v=7RgyLDVlAg4
4. svevind.com/media/
5. www.vogelbescherming.nl/actueel/bericht/5-vragen-over-windenergie-en-vogels#:~:text=Vulnerable%20birds%20on%20land,and%20plovers%2C%20cranes%20and%20gulls
6. rainforestjournalismfund.org/stories/how-wind-power-tree-driving-deforestation-amazon
7. www.noordzeeloket.nl/en/functions-and-use/offshore-wind-energy/ecology/offshore-wind-ecological-programme-wozep/
8. www.wur.nl/en/research-results/research-institutes/environmental-research/show-wenr/effect-of-wind-turbines-on-bird-mortality-often-underestimated.htm
9. Article "Mortality limits used in wind energy impact assessment underestimate impacts of wind farms on bird populations," Ecology and Evolution Volume 10, July 2020; research.wur.co.uk/en/publications/mortality-limits-used-in-wind-energy-impact-assessment-underestimate
10. Article "Red Kite seriously threatened by wind turbines," Chris van Deursen, 2014
11. Statement of Scope and Detail - NRD, March 29, 2023; www.reswestoverijssel.nl/planmer/nrd/default.aspx

12. Article "Bats Killed in Large Numbers at United States Wind Energy Facilities" by Hayes in BioScience, Volume 63, Issue 12, December 2013
13. Article "Comparing bird and bat fatality-rate estimates among North American wind-energy projects" by Smallwood in Wildlife Society Bulletin Volume 37, issue 1, March 2013
14. Article "Dogs Detect Larger Wind Energy Effects on Bats and Birds" by Smallwood et al, The Journal of Wildlife Management 1-13; 2020
15. Article "Multiple mortality events in bats: A global review" by O'shea et al., in Mammal review, Feb. 2016
16. Article Wind Turbines as Landscape Impediments to the Migratory Connectivity of Bats by Paul.M. Cryan, 2011, pubs.er.usgs.gov/publication/70003579
17. Article "Bats in the Anthropocene: Conservation of Bats in a Changing World," Voigt et al., 2016
18. Article "Wind turbines without curtailment produce large numbers of bat fatalities throughout their lifetime: A call against ignorance and neglect," Global Ecology and Conservation Volume 37, September 2022
19. klimaatweb.nl/policy/answers-to-room-questions-about-the-death-of-a-lammergier-after-collision-with-a-dutch-windmill/
20. www-klimaatfeiten-nl.translate.goog/maatregelen/milieu-aspecten/fauna?_x_tr_sl=nl&_x_tr_tl=en&_x_tr_hl=nl
21. Article "More than 75 percent decline over 27 years in total flying insect biomass in protected areas," Caspar A. Hallman et al., October 2017; journals.plos.org/plosone/article?id=10.1371/journal.pone.0185809
22. Article "Interference of Flying Insects and Wind Parks (FliWip)" - Study Report, October 2018; www.dlr.de/tt/Portaldata/41/Resources/dokumente/st/FliWip-Final-Report.pdf
23. energy.ec.europa.eu/topics/infrastructure/high-level-groups/north-seas-energy-cooperation_en
24. map.4coffshore.com/offshorewind/
25. nos.nl/news-hour/article/2280296-northsea-becomes-big-building-place-for-windmills
26. The North Sea Foundation; www.noordzee.nl
27. www.wozep.nl
28. Report "Benthic development in and around offshore wind farm Princess Amalia Wind Park near the Dutch coastal zone before and after construction (2003-2017)"; Rijkswaterstaat, Amsterdam, April 29, 2018
29. www.fisheries.noaa.gov/national/marine-life-distress/2016-2023-humpback-whale-unusual-mortality-event-along-atlantic-coast
30. Article "200 kHz Commercial Sonar Systems Generate Lower Frequency Side Lobes Audible to Some Marine Mammals," Z. Daniel Deng et al., April 2014; journals.plos.org/plosone/article?id=10.1371/journal.pone.0095315
31. www.cfact.org/2022/07/26/threat-to-endangered-whales-gets-louder/
32. TNO report TNO 2021 R12503, "Kader Ecologie en Cumulatie 2021 (KEC 4.0) – zeezoogdieren", Januaryi 2022; https://publications.tno.nl/publication/34639149/3I2MVC/TNO-2021-R12503.pdf
33. vissersbond.nl/wp-content/uploads/2019/03/Cables-and-Pipes-on-the-North-Sea-2.png
34. Environmental impact study of cables and pipelines Wadden area, by Arcadis, August 2013; www.rvo.nl/sites/default/files/2016/09/Milieueffectstudie%20Kabels%20en%20Leidingen%20Waddenzee%20_%20Redactie_klein.pdf
35. www.wur.nl/en/show-longread/electromagnetic-fields-around-wind-farm-power-cables.htm

36. Article "The Effects of Anthropogenic Electromagnetic Fields (EMF) on the Early Development of Two Commercially Important Crustaceans, European Lobster, Homarus gammarus (L.) and Edible Crab, Cancer pagurus (L.); Journal of Marine Science and Engineering 2022, 10(5), 564; doi.org/10.3390/jmse10050564
37. www.knmi.nl/over-het-knmi/nieuws/windparken-mengen-zich-in-het-weer
38. wins50.co.uk
39. Article "Diurnal and seasonal variations of wind farm impacts on land surface temperature over western Texas. Climate dynamics 41(2): 307-326."; Zhou, L., Tian, Y., Roy, S.B., Dai, Y. and Chen, H. (2012)
40. sciencefiles.org/2023/05/01/climawandel-windparks-verursachen-trockenheit-und-duerre-die-belege-werden-immer-zahlreicher-neue-studie/
41. www.rivm.nl/sites/default/files/2020-09/Factsheet%20laagfrequent%20geluid.pdf
42. www.bnnvara.nl/zembla/artikelen/geluidsoverlast-door-windmolens-dit-is-wat-zembla-erover-ontdekte
43. www.vpro.nl/argos/lees/onderwerpen/windmolens/2020/onhoorbaar-geluid-schadelijk-voor-gezondheid.html
44. nos.nl/op3/artikel/2196081-een-aanval-met-onhoorbaar-geluid-hoe-werkt-dat
45. www.youtube.com/watch?v=LQCVX7NQ66M
46. https://radar.avrotros.nl/nieuws/item/huizen-bij-windmolens-dalen-38-in-waarde-dit-is-de-impact-in-jouw-buurt/
47. TNO report TNO 2022 P10374; "De verwachte impact van windturbines op huizenprijzen in Nederland. Een ruimtelijke analyse voor de periode 2020-2030", 3 March 2022
48. www.ipcc.ch/site/assets/uploads/2018/03/TAR-04.pdf
49. Article "Evaluation of SF6 Leakage from Gas Insulated Equipment on Electricity Networks in Great Britain," Philip Widger, 2018; www.mdpi.com/1996-1073/11/8/2037
50. Report SF6 emission, report number 19-0701; "SF6 emissie netbeheerders elektriciteit 2018", netbeheer Nederland, June 2019; https://www.netbeheernederland.nl/_upload/Files/SF6-emissie_netbeheerders_elektriciteit_2018_(rapport)_160.pdf
51. www-wind--watch-org.translate.goog/news/2019/10/29/windmolen-lekt-extreem-schadelijk-gas-windmills-leak-very-dangerous-gas/print/?_x_tr_sl=nl&_x_tr_tl=en&_x_tr_hl=nl
52. dilo.com/blog/article/alternatives-to-sf6-gas-what-are-the-available-options
53. Report "Chemical study on Bisphenol A", report number RIKZ/2001.027, July 2001
54. Report "Leading Edge erosion and pollution from wind turbine blades" by Asbjørn Solberg, Bård-Einar Rimereit en Jan Erik Weinbach; https://docs.wind-watch.org/Leading-Edge-erosion-and-pollution-from-wind-turbine-blades_5_july_English.pdf
55. www.chemanalyst.com/industry-report/bisphenol-a-market-57
56. WHO report "State of the science of endocrine disrupting chemicals 2012"; www.who.int/publications/i/item/9789241505031
57. www.efsa.europa.eu/en/topics/topic/bisphenol
58. www.dwarsliggers.eu/index.php/28-economie/918-wordt-bisfenol-a-de-pfos-van-de-windenergie
59. Article "Bisphenol A Induces Superfeminization in the Ramshorn Snail (Gastropoda: Prosobranchia) at Environmentally Relevant Concentrations", October 2005; https://www.ncbi.nlm.nih.gov/pmc/articles/PMC1874184/
60. renews.biz/32801/london-array-braced-for-blade-fix/
61. www.offshorewind.biz/2018/04/26/siemens-gamesa-starts-repairing-anholt-blades-london-array-up-next/

62. www.rtvnoord.nl/nieuws/983527/anne-wil-komt-met-schrik-vrij-op-n992-krijg-je-zon-brok-ijs-op-je-kop-dan-ben-je-dood
63. projects.oregonlive.com/wind-farms/?e
64. Federal Energy Regulatory Commission; www.ferc.gov
65. www.windpowermonthly.com/article/1793389/nordex-turbine-collapses-new-rwe-wind-farm-sweden
66. energyfactor.exxonmobil.eu/science-technology/lubricant-wind-turbines/
67. Article 'Costs of repair of wind turbine blades: Influence of technology aspects', Leon Mishnaevsky Jr., Department of Wind Energy, Technical University of Denmark, June 2020
68. stopshesethings.com/2021/12/23/busted-government-fines-another-wind-turbine-blade-recycler-for-illegal-dumping/.
69. ktxs.com/news/local/old-windfarm-blades-causing-problems-in-nolan-county
70. www.vestas.com/en/media/company-news/2023/vestas-unveils-circularity-solution-to-end-landfill-for-c3710818
71. Factsheet research "Hidden interests in wind turbine literature," Joris J. van Hoof, October 2021; www.windwiki.nl/wp-content/uploads/2021/10/2021-Factsheet-UTwente-Windturbines-van-Hoof.pdf

Fig. 6.18-19: Should we just get used to a horizon full of wind turbines both on land and at sea?
After all, millions more need to be built globally…

Thank you

Writing this book I had a fantastic time, thanks to my dear wife Mona. She provided me the stability and the peace to be able to do this.

Towards the end of the book, I involved my children in the writing process by summarizing some topics from the book for them or reading a bit aloud. The feedback I got from them - honest and wonderful adolescents - made me realize that I was on the right track.

Many thanks go to my former colleague Dr Coen Vermeeren. He helped me enormously with both the book's readability and the entire layout.

I also thank wind energy experts Ronald van Amelrooij and Fred Udo for their valuable comments and feedback.

Finally, I thank you, the reader, for reading this book. With the information provided, I hope to have given you tools and confidence for having discussions about energy transition and the use or location of wind turbines.

Like me, a growing group of people want to return to a life that focuses on basic human needs: food, water, and a roof over your head. Above all, this group of people also wants a society where love for each other and for nature is central and everyone's qualities are used to serve each other. Large-scale wind turbines are not needed for that. The fertile land on which they are put on can then be used to build small houses, large vegetable gardens and food forests.

(Re)developing the use of free energy, rather than wind and solar power, can also help take care of the earth in this respect. Thus, a world can emerge in which thinking and acting from abundance is central.

Glossary

Shaft height - The height of the axis of the wind turbine from the ground.

Biolab - A laboratory for biological research.

Capacity factor - The capacity factor is a measure of a wind turbine's productivity. It is the ratio between the actual electricity production of a wind turbine and the maximum possible output in the same period.

Carbon credits - Carbon credits, also called CO_2 dues, work like letters of permission for emissions. When a company buys CO_2 credits, usually from the government, it gets permission to generate one ton of CO_2 emissions. With carbon credits, carbon revenues flow vertically from companies to regulators, although companies that have excess credits can sell them to other companies.

CBDC - Central Bank Digital Currency; digital central bank money.

Club of Rome - The Club of Rome is a private foundation established in April 1968 by European scientists and entrepreneurs to highlight their concerns about the future of the world. The Club of Rome has issued several reports on the environment, the best known of which is "The Limits to Growth."

Cp performance coefficient - A factor indicating the maximum amount of energy a wind turbine can extract from the airstream.

Crumb motor - A special motor that ensures that the nacelle is always positioned so that the rotor blades face the wind.

Dynamo - A machine in which mechanical energy, entering through a rotating shaft, is converted into electrical energy.

Ecosystem - An ecosystem is a system consisting of the entirety of animals and plants found in a given area.

Exploitation - Running and earning from a business or property.

GWh - Gigawatt hour, a unit of labor or electrical energy, equal to 1.000.000.000 watt-hours.

Hedge fund - A hedge fund or leveraged fund is a mutual fund that is open to a limited number of investors and allowed by the financial authorities to employ a greater number of strategies than a regular mutual fund.

Installed Power - Installed power is the maximum capacity (of a generating unit) that can be utilized to supply electrical energy under rated conditions.

IPCC - An intergovernmental body of the United Nations tasked with advancing scientific knowledge about climate change caused by human activities.

KNMI - Abbreviation for Royal Netherlands Meteorological Institute.

kWh - Kilowatt hour, a unit of labor or electrical energy, equal to 3.600.000 J.

Monopile - This is basically a single, very large pile that is driven straight down and sticks into the ground like an oversized nail. Monopiles are mostly used when water is involved.

MSM - MainStream Media, or mainstream news sources such as the Dutch RTL4, SBS6, NPO as well as newspapers under the management of DPG Media.

MW - Megawatt, a unit of power, 1 MW equals 1 million watts.

NRD - Scope and Detail Memorandum. A document that underlies a Plan EIA and provides the framework for designating areas where solar and wind farms are to be located.

PFOS - PFOS (perfluorooctane sulfonates) is one chemical within the PFAS group, used to make products such as textiles water- and dirt-repellent.

EIR plan - A plan EIR or plan environmental impact report is an environmental impact report (EIR) accompanying a plan or program to be adopted.

Power station - English word for power plant.

Project EIR - A "project environmental impact report" (project EIR) is prepared before a permit is granted for the potentially harmful activities.

RES - Abbreviation of Regional Energy Strategy. The Netherlands is divided into 30 regions. Each region is represented by Provincial Council deputies, municipalities, water boards and energy companies. The 30 regions have been made responsible for implementing climate policy.

RIVM - Abbreviation for Dutch National Institute of Public Health and the Environment.

Sonar - (sound navigation and ranging) is a technique that uses sound to navigate underwater or detect other objects.

Sustainable - In the context of the climate as well as the global policies being rolled out on humanity by governments, it is good to take a moment to consider the term sustainable. You hear this term passed around daily these days. And if one day you don't hear it, it will appear in front of you somewhere on paper.

The fifth edition of the Dikke Van Dale - from 1914 - defines "sustainable" as "suitable, destined to last a long time. As an example, "this fabric is very durable," meaning "can last a long time. Now we make a leap in time". On NOS Teletext on October 22, 2016, there is a report 'More sustainable food sold'. The text shows that it is not about food that has a long shelf life, but about meat, vegetables and dairy products that have been produced in a way that preserves the environment. You wouldn't have figured this out with the 1914 Van Dale, but the fifteenth edition from 2015 does, because it includes the additional meaning of "sustainable": "using as few resources as possible; using renewable resources".

This modern meaning of "sustainable" has become so prominent that the original meaning "long-lasting" has been subsumed, which sometimes leads you astray. Regarding the redevelopment of a recreation area, the Internet reports, "The work consists of the reconstruction of paths. These will be replaced by concrete paths. This material is sustainable, requires little maintenance and thus lasts a long time". 'Sustainable concrete'. A lot of people will now be involuntarily tempted to think, "hey, so apparently that's good for the environment, that concrete". And perhaps that is exactly the association that the writer of this wants to elicit from us.

The term sustainable is widely used today and, as indicated, the word is associated with something good, namely a better environment. Thus, the original meaning of this word has been deliberately modified in the Dictionary.

If you look at the term sustainable in a different way, it becomes clear that it is a cleverly chosen term, behind which there is a hidden agenda. The term is thus appropriate, in accordance with its original meaning, because many people worship the sustainability agenda.

Theoretically generated amount of energy - Theoretical maximum amount of energy that can be generated, determined by the technology used in combination with predicted average wind power on site.

Tip height - The height of a wind turbine from the ground to the tip of the rotor blade, when in the vertical up position.

Ton - One ton is equivalent to 1.000 kilograms.

TWh - Terrawatt-hour, a unit of labor or electrical energy, equal to 1.000.000.000.000 watt-hours or 3.6 PetaJoules (PJ).

Full load hour - A full-load hour is a unit for the effective output of an energy source. The number of full-load hours can be thought of as the length of time during which the energy source effectively produced energy at full power.

Read more

Websites

- www.stopthesethings.com
- www.cfact.org
- www.wind-watch.org
- www.wattsupwiththat.com

And my website
- www.metdewindmee.com

Photos

All images and photographs used in this book are from free platforms such as Wikipedia, Wikimedia, pixabay.com and pxhere.com, unless otherwise indicated.

Offshore Wind Park Amrumbank West, the German part of the North Sea.

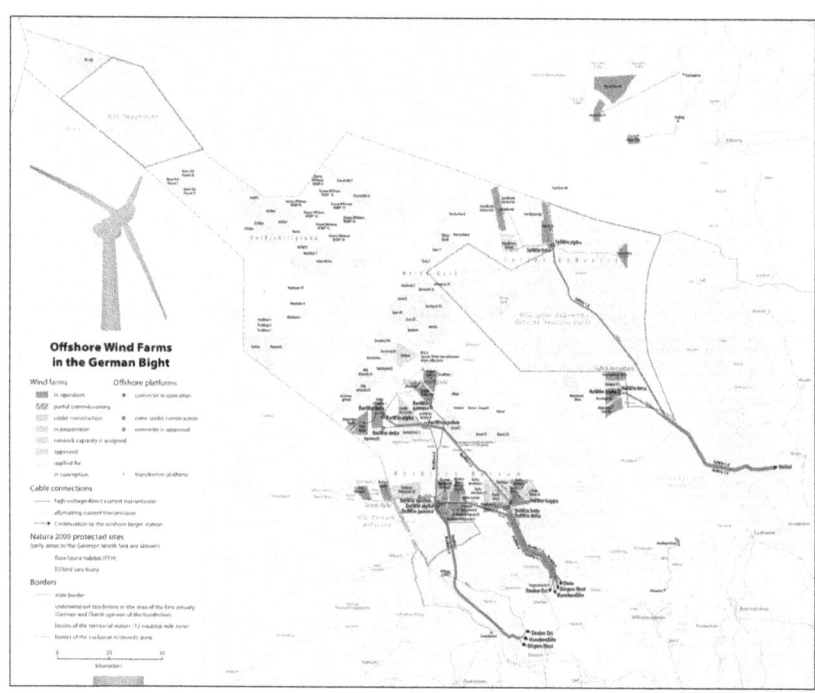
Germany also wants to fill the North Sea with wind turbines.

About the author

In the late 1970s I was born in Hellendoorn, a small village in Salland, Overijssel, on the edge of Twente. The village was characterized by the presence of 2 authentic windmills that performed the function of grain mills. During my childhood years, one of the two windmills was still active and selling flour. I loved coming there and was impressed by this technical construction work.

My childhood was a time when people still watched a black and white picture tube through the antenna. Computers and the Internet did not exist yet. Every day I spent time outside with friends, no matter what the weather was. My life revolved around outdoor activities. I also helped out in my parents' vegetable garden - many people back then still had vegetable gardens to grow their own vegetables. At that time we were inventive and creative, we were on our own and developed as we learned from nature and how to interact with nature. Unforced and pure. It was a period of timeless and boundless discovery and experience. Breathing the fresh air every day, through all weathers, with a life energy that you felt flowing throughout the day. What a wonderful time it was. And then the high school years arrived. Without realizing it at the time, I was sucked into a system. I became convinced that I needed a diploma to get a job and build a future for myself. Programmed and not realizing the system behind this, the bond between me and nature further crumbled. The free enjoyment and discovery of and with nature during this period gave way to studying and working to pay the rent. Over time, I began to ask myself what made me go along with this system for so long. Doesn't nature have everything needed to live a beautiful and happy life? Then why was that taken away from me? Why did I allow that to happen?

In recent years, my life path has become much clearer and my developments have accelerated. Being as self-sufficient as possible without the burdens of the current system is what I am working toward. The connection with nature and the whole universe has landed again in my own system. In this, I have been helped by all the beautiful people who have come my way over the past few years. With a technical background as an Aerospace Engineer, specialized in Engineering of lightweight materials and associated manufacturing processes for the production of lightweight structures in the aircraft industry, I have the necessary technical interfaces with the technology used in modern wind turbines. I wrote this book from my heart, out of love for humanity and nature. From my childlike nature, I started writing uninhibitedly about the devastating impact of the climate agenda on society and nature, and specifically about wind turbines. To be able to share this information with you feels to me like an important step in my process to living self-sufficiently in and with nature.

Morning mist at Te Apiti Wind Farm in New Zealand.
Pristine nature can be removed from our dictionary... Or rather not!

www.ingramcontent.com/pod-product-compliance
Lightning Source LLC
LaVergne TN
LVHW081538070526
838199LV00056B/3703